FRONTIER CABIN STORY

FRONTIER CABIN STORY

The Rediscovered History
—— *of a* ——
West Virginia Log Farmhouse

JOSEPH GOSS

A PEACE CORPS WRITERS BOOK

Frontier Cabin Story:

The Rediscovered History of a West Virginia Log Farmhouse

A Peace Corps Writers Book – an imprint of Peace Corps Worldwide

Printed in the United States of America

by Peace Corps Writers of Oakland, California

Front Cover: *West Virginia Farmhouse*, watercolor by Lynne F. Goss.
Back Cover: *Winter Sunrise over the Blue Ridge*, watercolor by Lynne F. Goss.
Cover designs: Eric D. Goss.

For more information, contact peacecorpsworldwide@gmail.com.

Peace Corps Writers and the Peace Corps Writers colophon are trademarks of PeaceCorpsWorldwide.org.

ISBN-13: 978-1-935925-95-8
Library of Congress Control Number: 2018914859

First Peace Corps Writers Edition, December 2018

*For all the uncelebrated individuals who
work to keep our cherished history
alive and early homes intact.*

CONTENTS

CONTENTS

FIGURES

ACKNOWLEDGEMENTS

THIS PROJECT MAY well not have taken flight without the abundance of resources available to me from the following organizations:

Berkeley County Clerk's Office
Berkeley County Historical Society (BCHS)
Historic Shepherdstown and Museum
Jefferson County Clerk's Office
Jefferson County Historic Landmarks Commission
Library of Congress—Chronicling America project
David M. Rubenstein Rare Book and Manuscript Library, Duke
    University
Ruth Scarborough Library, Shepherd University
Shepherdstown Library

I want to thank the following individuals for their generous help:

R. Todd Funkhouser, president of BCHS, who oriented me to the Society's vast collection of materials, showed me how to use them, and suggested explanations for contradictory information.

Christine Toms, former special collections librarian, and digital initiatives and website manager at the Scarborough Library, who guided me through Shepherd University's valuable collection of historical Jefferson County and West Virginia archival materials. Her enthusiasm for and encouragement of this work and her reading of the manuscript were invaluable.

John C. Allen Jr., architectural historian and past chair of the Jefferson County Historic Landmarks Commission. Mr. Allen visited our log farmhouse and offered valuable information about its architectural details and probable age. His book, *Uncommon Vernacular: The Early Houses of Jefferson County, West Virginia, 1735–1835*, provided a wealth of material and stimulus for this project. Furthermore, I am grateful for his cloquent foreword.

Dr. Jerry B. Thomas, Historic Shepherdstown and Museum, who afforded access to the irreplaceable 1795–1796 Selby dry goods store account book and other singular materials for my review.

ACKNOWLEDGEMENTS

Lynne F. Goss, my wife and fervent disciple of English literature, who reviewed and edited the manuscript numerous times. Her unfailing eye for hyperbole has saved me from many minor embarrassments. She created the enchanting front and back cover art as well.

Frank Thomas, Ph.D., adjunct professor of English and American Studies, University of Connecticut, retired. Dr. Thomas's thoughtful reading of the entire manuscript has quietly helped me see problems I could not.

Eric D. Goss, my son and graphic designer, who designed the front and back covers and much more. He set the formatting for the entire manuscript, helped create several of the illustrations, and sharpened many of the photographs and drawings. His design and publishing skills made it possible for me to translate this project into its final printed form.

FOREWORD

HISTORIC HOUSES ARE useful relics. Not only do these buildings provide sturdy shelter for those of us in the present, but they also hold a store of features that can convey the sweep of history to anyone willing to look closely. Crafted by the local culture, the early houses of Jefferson County, West Virginia, embody the history of the place over time. Each of these homes has the ability to teach us of our shared past. Too often, however, the intricate histories of these buildings remain hidden to those who pass by them daily, and even to those who live inside them. These silent witnesses wait patiently to tell their remarkable stories.

Joseph Goss has given voice to the historic log house that his family has lovingly preserved. His meticulously detailed history of this farmhouse allows the building to share its intimate tales. The farm's history is enhanced with Goss's detailed accounts of the larger narratives of Shepherdstown, Jefferson County, Colonial Virginia, and West Virginia. With the aid of this bounding context, the story of one house becomes something larger. Goss shows the interwoven nature of history through his well-researched narrative of this humble, log house.

As someone who values historic buildings, especially those in Jefferson County, I applaud Goss for writing this architectural biography. He and his family strive to preserve their home for future generations while promoting a better understanding of its place in the rich tapestry of our local history.

John C. Allen Jr., architectural historian

CHAPTER 1 INTRODUCTION

THIS STORY BEGINS with a couple, on the threshold of retirement, searching for something more fulfilling in life. For several years my wife, Lynne, and I had been looking for an old country place to serve as a refuge from the frenzied multitudes near Washington, D.C., and to afford closer contact with nature.

Unexpectedly, a stunning historic log farmhouse near Shepherdstown in the Eastern Panhandle of West Virginia came to the market. It struck us at once with the views it commanded of the ageless Blue Ridge and its carefully restored historical elements. It stood atop a serenely beautiful ten-acre property still surrounded by working farmlands as it was over 200 years ago. In June 2011, we overcame our initial panic about owning and managing such an expansive property and bought the old place.

This bold step changed our lives in countless ways. It has tested our self-reliance. We have faced freezing nights without heat, frozen pipes, massive termite and stink bug infestations, basement floods, a lightning strike, mysterious odors, giant escaped snapping turtles, and a deserted pasture crying out for livestock to gorge on its out-of-control brush. The reward for overcoming all these troubles was getting to know Appalachian people and their generosity, resourcefulness, humor, kindness, tolerance of eccentricity, and in some cases, perseverance through real hardship. The lives of our wild mammalian, avian, amphibian, and aquatic residents and visitors never stop captivating us. Our children, extended family, and friends have paid us many delightful visits here, making it a gathering place for those we love.

In many ways, this house reminded us of the eighteenth-century colonial farmhouse Lynne's parents owned for forty years near Henniker, New Hampshire. We spent many summer weekends there while raising our children in Lexington, Massachusetts. It was heart-rending to sell the old house once Lynne's parents grew too old to maintain it. Our own eighteenth-century home now incorporates a few keepsakes from the Henniker house creating a tangible bond between them. We hope that our grandchildren will come to love and use our Shepherdstown home as our children did their grandparents' New Hampshire place.

FRONTIER CABIN STORY

An unanticipated bonus of purchasing the farmhouse was that it coincided with Lynne's taking up watercolor painting. The house, a neighbor's antique barn and cattle, and the endlessly shifting landscape provide her with rich material to paint. Our home now displays many of these works—an artistic record of the farm to parallel this written one. The lovely watercolors on the front and back covers showing the farmhouse's east façade and the Blue Ridge Mountains in winter are Lynne's paintings.

People told us that our log house dated from 1780, which would make it one of the oldest homes in the vicinity and of inherent historical worth. During our first few years of ownership, we occupied ourselves with projects in and around the house, including a significant addition to the first floor, which we hoped might allow us to age in place. With these projects behind us by 2015, my curiosity about the received date of 1780 caught up with me.

Such an early date, especially in West Virginia, which drew settlers later than states along the coast, is suspect since owners of ancient houses will occasionally inflate their age. Thus, I began to research the epoch, early owners, and history of the home. I believe the past owners and residents are an essential part of the history, spirit, and energy of the house. I hope that this project will honor them and the other pioneers, both men and women, European and enslaved African American, who settled the frontier. Over the lifetime of this project, I have come to appreciate them and this ancient dwelling profoundly, and its endurance inspires me.

Another goal I have is to educate ourselves and future owners of our farmhouse. Further, I hope to contribute something original about the history of Shepherdstown, a community that has greatly enriched our lives.

Before going further, I want readers to know that much of what follows, especially in some of the later chapters, contains extensive historical detail. Even so, there are humorous scenes and much absorbing material about our subjects' lives. I trust readers will find this material engaging by how much of it has completely disappeared from local memory and how it gives us a grasp on the concerns of people far from us in time but who inhabited the same places we do today. Also, for sincere seekers of the obscure, to my knowledge, no one has ever before published the material I have obtained from primary sources.

I began this project hoping to portray the historical record of one long-overlooked farmhouse and all that I could learn about the people with connections to it. And that is how it has culminated. But I also want it to serve as a useful reference for disciples of local history. I believe the type of research I have done and the results I achieved are unique for such an undocumented place, at least in the Shepherdstown area. It may work too as a prototype for researchers of forgotten archaic homes anywhere. Without a doubt, it shows how much you can find out about even the least-known places if you are willing to search relentlessly for it.

In the spirit of self-disclosure, I am an environmental engineer, not a trained historian. Nevertheless, I think some of the analytical methods I use in engineering practice were beneficial in executing this project.

In the beginning, I thought this endeavor might be a simple matter of visiting the Jefferson County courthouse to look up a few past deeds to the property. Instead, to my surprise it turned into a labyrinthine odyssey, which eventually led me to realize my original aims and much more. Along the way, I learned much about the history of Shepherdstown and the region, allowing me to see our farmhouse in the context of its period and setting.

We still know too little about the early occupants of our farmhouse, although we know some of their names and have fragments of their stories. I have tried to fill these gaps with details of its better-documented absentee owners' and their families' lives. In some cases, I have used parallel accounts about nearby places with similar historical situations.

I ask readers to trust that what I have chosen to write about gave me a better understanding of the farmhouse and made this project more interesting than merely learning the names and dates connected with it. The unplanned by-product of this approach has been to rediscover the lives of some of the long-forgotten but prominent early citizens of Shepherdstown. Thus, their vanished lives can again briefly occupy our attention, and perhaps some residents of present-day Shepherdstown will come to know them for the first time.

I am grateful to the many people I met with a passion for local history without whose resources, insights, and encouragement I could not have completed this work. Although there will always be more sources I could pursue, I have explored much farther than I originally planned and far surpassed my original goals. If a future researcher is interested in learning still more about this long-overlooked and venerable old house, its owners, residents, and enslaved workers, or its connection with the surrounding area, I hope my findings will give them a head start.

That first innocent visit to the Jefferson County courthouse quickly turned into a dead end when I could only trace the property deeds for the old farmhouse back to 1914. The 1914 deed simply divided a 596-acre tract of land between its two owners—Eliza Williamson, who received 275 acres including the farmhouse and her sister, Florence Shepherd, who got the remaining 321 acres.[1]

Since the 1914 deed gave no information about earlier owners, I decided to try to trace the property from its earliest documentation forward in time. Using this approach, I found a map through the Jefferson County Historic Landmarks Commission's *wvgeohistory.org* website showing the boundaries of all the eighteenth-century royal patents and land grants in Jefferson County superimposed on a modern-day map.[2] The relevant part of this map appears in Figure 1.1. The log farmhouse's position on the modern map is within the boundaries of Colonel William David Morgan's September 14, 1756, 300-acre grant from Thomas Fairfax of "waste and ungranted land," in the legal instrument's wording.[3]

I found another critical piece of information on the Library of Congress's website. It was an 1852 tax map of Jefferson County drawn by S. Howell Brown. This map shows our house situated on a large tract then owned by Walter B. Selby—illustrated in Figure 1.2.[4] Thinking that Walter Selby could be the first owner and builder of the house, I started researching

---

1   Jefferson County Clerk, *Deed Book 110*, Page 316, January 8, 1914.

2   West Virginia GeoHistory/Geoexplorer Project, "Jefferson County Land Grants," 2010. Retrieved from http://wvgeohistory.org/portals/0/ESRIJavascriptMaps /GHLandGrants/viewer/index.html

3   Northern Neck Grants, *Book H*, Page 675, Virginia State Library, September 14, 1756. Retrieved from http://www.wvgeohistory.org

4   Brown, S. Howell, "Map of Jefferson County, West Virginia," 1883, Library of Congress. Retrieved from https://www.loc.gov/resource/g3893j.la001395/

early deeds and genealogies in Berkeley and Jefferson counties to see if either Colonel William Morgan's or Walter B. Selby's ownership of the house could have been chronologically possible around 1780. Given the house's alleged construction date of 1780, the earliest deeds to its land—if there were any—ought to be found in Berkeley County, from which Jefferson County split off in 1801.

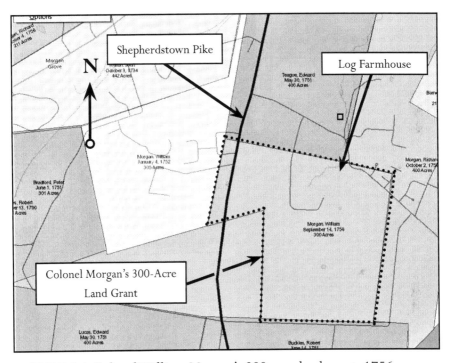

FIGURE 1.1 Colonel William Morgan's 300-acre land grant, 1756.
Image courtesy of the West Virginia GeoExplorer Project.

Internet genealogical research showed that Colonel Morgan lived between 1723 and 1788 and Walter Selby between 1770 and 1855.[5] An explanation is in order about people's birth and death years, which I cite throughout this volume. I obtained most of them from the *familysearch.org* website of the Church of Jesus Christ of Latter-Day Saints (LDS). Although its information is not always accurate, it includes an immense number of names and dates, and I believe it to be more reliable than many other

5   The Church of Jesus Christ of Latter-day Saints, "Ancestral File," database, FamilySearch, entry for Sgt. Major Richard Morgan, 2015. Retrieved from https://familysearch.org/ark:/61903/2:1:MWS3-HF1

internet sources. I also located some people's years on other internet sites if they were not on the LDS site. Still others came from a family tree found in the archives of the Historic Shepherdstown Museum.

It is possible that Colonel Morgan could have built the house, although he was already fifty-seven years old in 1780. Walter Selby is unlikely to have owned or built the log house around 1780 since he was only ten years old at that time. My research also revealed that Walter Selby married Colonel Morgan's daughter, Eleanor, in 1797. This fact could signal that the newly married couple might have built the house much later than 1780.[6,7]

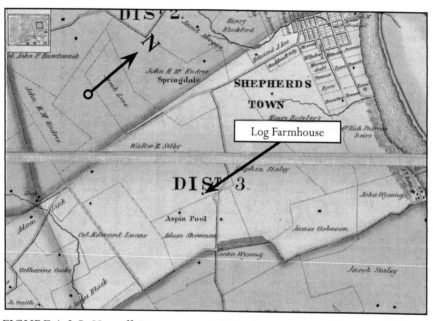

FIGURE 1.2 S. Howell Brown map, 1852. *Image courtesy of the West Virginia GeoExplorer Project.*

I will put off a detailed physical description of the farmhouse and how it has changed over time until close to the end of the book. Thus the reader will first have got a sense of its historical context and the people connected

---

6 Historic Shepherdstown & Museum, "Shepherdstown 250 Parade: Family History Descriptions," November 11, 2012. Retrieved from http://historicshepherdstown.com /shep250_parade.htm

7 Keesecker, Guy L., compiler and editor, "Index," *Marriage Records of Berkeley County for the Period of 1781–1854*, 1969, 200.

with it. After becoming familiar with its owners and occupants, the reader will perhaps better understand its modifications and extensions.

Walter Selby was a prosperous dry goods merchant in Shepherdstown by the mid-1790's, and in 1810 he bought the Wynkoop Tavern located a block from his business on German Street.[8,9] Selby's purchase of the tavern confirms that he was not a farmer and that he owned a grand house in town much more elegant than our humble log farmhouse. I could not precisely determine where the Selbys lived before 1810, but his occupation almost rules out a simple farmhouse.

The question of who owned or lived in the rustic log house between 1780 and 1810, if it dates from this period, vexed me for months. I found no deeds in the Berkeley County deed books related to the property from 1780 to 1801. However, Walter Selby was the grantee on many deeds in Berkeley and Jefferson Counties from 1797 through 1836, owning over 600 acres at his death in 1855. The grantors of some of these deeds were heirs of Colonel Morgan.

Although I obtained copies of all these deeds and others early on in my research, I delayed reading most of them due to the difficulty of transcribing their often barely legible longhand script. Once understood, these deeds did reveal part of the provenance of the log farmhouse. I will return to them later in this story. Extracts of all the deeds I read appear in the appendices.

Five months after beginning this investigation, I started to believe I might never know who the earliest owner or builder of our house was. Scouring the bottom of the document barrel, I decided to review some obscure Morgan and Selby family file folders in the locked vault room at the Berkeley County Historical Society. I had known about them at the outset of my research, but they did not seem to be particularly good prospects at the time. What I found was a crucial page of handwritten research notes. Like the Rosetta Stone, which held the key to deciphering Egyptian hieroglyphs, these notes allowed me to connect Colonel William

---

8   Pendleton, Helen Boteler, "The Wynkoop, Morgan, Selby, Hamtramck Families," *Magazine of the Jefferson County Historical Society*, Charles Town, West Virginia, Vol. VIII, December 1942, 10.
9   Jefferson County Clerk, *Deed Book 6*, Pages 168–170, September 20, 1810.

FRONTIER CABIN STORY

Morgan's 1788 will with the 1852 tax map revealing the first owner of the log farmhouse.[10] Yet, I had almost missed this pivotal discovery. A special boon of this finding is that the earliest owners of our place and those closely connected with them represented some of Shepherdstown's foremost families. Read on to learn more.

Before continuing, I offer a quotation from a compilation of the early marriage records of Berkeley County, which befits some of the first settlers of this region—a few of whom we are about to meet:

> As we turn the page and meet for the first time the families represented here, let us stop and reflect. These were the people who faced the wilderness with all its hardship, all its horror, and all its uncertainty. They settled the land and made it fruitful, formed religious principles that have stood the test and conquered the tremendous problems of transportation and endured the ruin of many wars. Their mechanical genius surprised the world. They have fought for the Rights of Common Man against the oppression of foreign influences. Theirs were the roots of western mankind which made America grow. West Virginians of every nationality, every race and every creed, we salute you![11]

---

10 Wood, Don C., research notes, undated. BCHS Survey File S-85.

11 Keesecker, Guy L., "Introduction to the Families," *Marriage Records of Berkeley County for the Period of 1781–1854,* 1969.

CHAPTER 2 EARLY SETTLEMENT

FOR MOST OF its recorded history the Shepherdstown, West Virginia, region—located in the Eastern Panhandle of the state— was part of the Virginia colony and later the Commonwealth of Virginia. Before colonization, missionary reports tell that Hurons lived in present-day West Virginia in the late 1500's and early 1600's. In the 1600's, the Iroquois Confederacy, headquartered in New York and made up of the Mohawk, Onondaga, Cayuga, Oneida, and Seneca tribes, forced the Hurons from the region.

The Iroquois Confederacy did not occupy the area but used it for hunting in spring and summer. The Shawnee, Mingo, and Delaware tribes also used the region as a hunting ground at that time. By the early 1700's, the Tuscarora lived in the Eastern Panhandle, but they moved north to New York and became the sixth nation admitted to the Iroquois Confederacy in 1712.[12] Hence, by that time few Native Americans resided in the northern Shenandoah Valley, a rough geographic match of the Eastern Panhandle.

Before 1728, the colonial government in Williamsburg restricted settlement west of the Blue Ridge Mountains to avoid conflict with Indian tribes. Conditions changed beginning in 1728 when the government granted the first lands in the Shenandoah Valley to check increasing Indian attacks in the Virginia Piedmont and to discourage fugitive slaves from the refuge they had found in mountain enclaves.[13] French intentions and activities further west might also have motivated the colonial government to populate the Shenandoah Valley.

J. E. Norris tells of new settlers who came to the area from Pennsylvania in about 1726 or 1727 and built a village named New Mecklenburg, after the place of their German origin.[14] A chronicler of Shepherdstown history, Danske Bedinger Dandridge, however, claims that Shepherdstown never went by the name New Mecklenburg. According to Dandridge, the name

---

12 Jefferson County Historic Landmarks Commission, "History of Jefferson County, West Virginia, Native American Habitation," 2006. Retrieved from http://jeffersonhistoricalwv.org/thehistory.html

13 Allen, John C. Jr., *Uncommon Vernacular*, West Virginia University Press, 2011, 24.

14 Norris, J. E., editor, *History of the Lower Shenandoah Valley Counties of Frederick, Berkeley, Jefferson and Clarke*, A. Warner & Co., 1890, 51.

Mecklenburg for today's Shepherdstown does not appear before the early 1760's. Before that, the village briefly went by the name Swearingen's Ferry and before that by the name Pack Horse Ford.[15,16] More on this subject will follow.

Joist—or Jost—Hite, a German immigrant, was among the first wave of pioneers to enter the Shenandoah Valley. He received large land grants and brought a group of families from Pennsylvania to the valley in 1731. Many settlers followed in 1731 and 1732.[17]

Though officially open to settlement in 1728, the Valley did not see a massive influx of European settlers until the mid-1700's. In 1744, the Colony of Virginia bought the Iroquois title to ownership of western Virginia in the Treaty of Lancaster, alerting the Indian tribes in the region to English intentions to settle the frontier. By contrast, the French were more interested in trading with the Indians than in populating the area. This situation inclined the Mingo tribe to support the French during the French and Indian War. Although the Iroquois Confederacy remained neutral, many of its tribes also allied with the French. Sadly for the Indians, the French lost the war and relinquished their eastern North American possessions to the English.[18]

The lands granted to the earliest settlers were by royal patent from the King. By the time settlement was promoted in earnest, Thomas Fairfax, the sixth Lord Fairfax of Cameron (1693–1781), had acquired the franchise to over five million acres in northern Virginia by inheritance originating from his maternal grandfather, Thomas Culpeper, the second Baron Culpeper (1635–1689). This land was the vast tract called the Northern Neck Proprietary of Virginia, displayed in Figure 2.1. The Northern Neck included the land bounded on the north by the Potomac River, on the south by the Rappahannock River, and on the west by the line between Augusta and Frederick Counties—the so-called Fairfax

---

15 Dandridge, Danske Bedinger, *Historic Shepherdstown*, The Michie Company, 1910, 50.
16 Dandridge, 278.
17 Stine, O. C., compiler, *Notes on Early Area History, The Land*, 1960, 1, Scarborough Library, Jefferson County Special Collection, Shepherd University.
18 Jefferson County Historic Landmarks Commission, "History of Jefferson County, West Virginia, The Eighteenth Century," 2016. Retrieved from http://jeffersoncountyhlc.org /index.php/education/history/

Line.[19] Shepherdstown lies in the far northeastern part of the Northern Neck.

The Acts of Virginia of 1713 compelled anyone receiving a land patent or grant to build "one good Dwelling-house after the Manner of Virginia

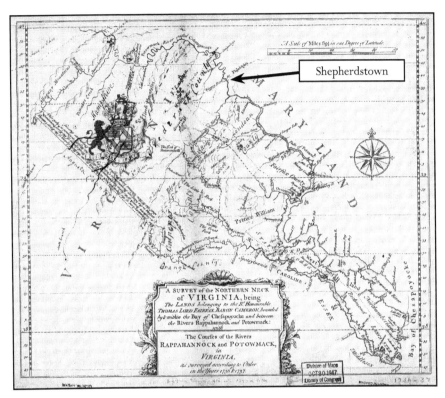

FIGURE 2.1 The Northern Neck of Virginia, 1736–1737 survey. *Image courtesy of Library of Congress Geography and Map Division.*

Building," of at least twenty feet by sixteen feet in size within three years, or the land must revert to the grantor.[20] The vast majority of the settlement houses and cabins have not survived due to deterioration, replacement, or outright removal. I have not seen documentary or physical evidence of a settlement cabin, if one existed, on Colonel William

19 Weisiger, Minor T., compiler, "Northern Neck Land Proprietary Records, Research Notes Number 23," The Library of Virginia, November 2002. Retrieved from http://www.lva.virginia.gov/public/guides/rn23_nneckland.pdf

20 Google Books, "Acts of Assembly, Passed in the Colony of Virginia: From 1662 to 1715," Volume 1, 2015. Retrieved from https://books.google.com

Morgan's original 1756 land grant where our log farmhouse stands now. I will touch on this again briefly in Chapter 5.

I do not believe the log farmhouse is the settlement cabin for this land grant, although it cannot be ruled out. In any case, it would have been larger than needed and built too late—if built around 1780—to meet the three-year time limit in the 1713 Acts of Virginia. Nonetheless, elements from an eradicated settlement cabin could have reappeared in our farmhouse. Reuse of dwelling materials was common and spoke of the settlers' frugality and conservation of precious resources. Hence, some of the early surviving houses of the Shepherdstown area could have more ancient parts than the owners suspect.

In 1734, Thomas Shepherd (1705–1776) obtained a 222-acre land patent on the south bank of the Potomac River. According to some sources, he planned to lay out a town and sell lots on fifty of those acres.[21,22] Shepherd purchased an additional fifty acres from Richard Morgan, Colonel Morgan's father. I will tell more about this purchase and its location relative to Shepherd's patent in Chapter 4.

The 1734 date of Shepherd's planning for a new town does not mean there were no settlers in or near the proposed town already. Previously, I have mentioned the possibility of colonizers in the area as early as the late 1720's. There is even documentation of Presbyterian settlers in the area as early as 1719 and a controversial tombstone near Duffields of a woman named Katerina Beierlin with the dates 1687–17[?]7. The questionable digit could be a zero or a five, although the year 1707 seems more likely, according to Theriault.[23] One source cites tombstone dates as early as 1720 in the German Reformed Church graveyard on East German Street, although I have not found them.[24]

In 1738 or 1739, Shepherd built the first of his grist mills along the Town Run. The mill, off of East High Street, still survives with its forty-foot

21 Brooke, R., "Facsimile of Original Survey for Thomas Shepherd," April 11, 1734. BCHS Morgan Family Files.
22 Gardiner, Mabel Henshaw and Gardiner, Ann Henshaw, *Chronicles of Old Berkeley, A Narrative History of a Virginia County from Its Beginnings to 1926*, The Seeman Press, 1938, 56.
23 Theriault, William D., *History of Eastern Jefferson County, West Virginia*, 1988, 7.
24 Dandridge, 15.

diameter water wheel—the largest overshot mill wheel in the world capable of operation at least until the 1990's.[25] The mill is now a private residence. At such an early date, there must have already been enough settlers in the area to need the services of a grist mill.[26] By 1762, many of the lot owners in Shepherd's hamlet wanted to live in an incorporated town. Therefore, Shepherd sent a bill to the House of Burgesses in Williamsburg to formally organize the settlement on November 12, 1762. The House passed the bill and incorporated the town as Mecklenburg.

No records attest to the reason for the choice of the town's name. However, some believe Charlottesville was to be its name to honor Queen Charlotte whom King George III had recently married. Fatefully, the city that became the familiar Charlottesville, Virginia, applied for incorporation earlier the same day in Williamsburg. Mecklenburg is the region in Germany where Queen Charlotte was born and from which some of Shepherdstown's earliest settlers came, as already mentioned. These facts may account for the town's first incorporated name.

The name Mecklenburg lasted until 1798 when the Virginia Assembly changed it to Shepherd's Town to honor its founder.[27] After incorporation, the town grew steadily. In 1762, it may have had a population of about 100. By 1804, the *American Gazetteer* reported it had 1,033 residents, mostly of German extraction.[28] The *American Gazetteer,* published in Boston and searchable on the Library of Congress's website, was a kind of encyclopedia of America.

The town's 2000 U.S. Census population of 803—a decline since 1804— did not include Shepherd University students. By 2010, its population had soared to 1,734 due to the town's annexation of the University's residence halls to achieve a more equitable allocation of tax revenues.[29]

---

25 The Historic Shepherdstown Commission, Inc., *See Shepherd's Town*, Volume III, 1997, 16, Scarborough Library, Jefferson County Special Collection, Shepherd University.

26 Kenamond, A. D., *Prominent Men of Shepherdstown During Its First 200 Years*, A Jefferson County Historical Society Publication, 1963, 11.

27 Kenamond, 12–13.

28 Stine, O. C., compiler, *Notes on Early Area History, Shepherdstown Population Through Two Centuries*, 1960, 1, Scarborough Library, Jefferson County Special Collection, Shepherd University.

29 Goodman, Rich, "Building Together for Mutual Benefit," *The Observer*, Shepherdstown, W. Va., July 2017, 7.

Curiously, Shepherdstown was one of many sites considered for the nation's new capital district in 1790. Leading citizens asked for subscriptions to defray the expenses of public buildings hoping to lure the authorities to fix the new capital at Shepherdstown. They hoped that the federal government would set up its permanent seat on the Maryland side of the Potomac River across from the town with half of the future ten-square-mile capital district situated on the Virginia side of the Potomac River.

A visit from President George Washington encouraged these hopes even though Washington had informed residents that other places along the Potomac had already made substantial offers. It was never likely that the $20,000 raised could have impressed the federal authorities.[30] It is amusing to think that the eventual District of Columbia encompassed ten square miles sited partly in Maryland, partly in Virginia, and that the Potomac River bisected it precisely as it would have at Shepherdstown.

Thomas Shepherd sold off for a profit the first ninety-six lots laid out for his town—each 103 feet wide by 206 feet long. Not to diminish his considerable historical importance, today we might consider Shepherd to have been a land developer or speculator. The price of a lot was five pounds, and ground rent was five shillings.[31] An Act of Virginia increased the number of lots to 202 in 1798.[32] The town charter stipulated that each buyer had to improve his lot with a "good dwelling," measuring at least twenty feet by seventeen feet within two years of acquisition or it would revert to the grantor. An 1873 plan of Shepherdstown showing all its 202 lots appears in Figure 2.2.[33]

Shepherdstown in the late eighteenth century must have looked vastly different from today if the earliest buildings followed the "good dwelling" prescription of the town's charter. Most of the original charter-mandated

---

30 Gardiner and Gardiner, 60–61.

31 Musser, Clifford S., *Two Hundred Years' History of Shepherdstown, 1730–1931*, Printed by the *Independent*, 1931, 11.

32 West Virginia GeoHistory Project, "Map Gallery, 1873 Shepherdstown," 2010. Retrieved from http://www.wvgeohistory.org/Portals/0/zoomify/URLDrivenPage .htm?zoomifyImagePath=/Portals/0/zoomify/Shepherdstown_Map_1873 &zoomifyInitialX=800&zoomifyInitialY=400&zoomifyInitialZoom=1 &zoomifyToolbarVisibility=1&zoomifyNavigatorVisibility=1

33 The Historic Shepherdstown Commission, Inc., xiii.

houses, as well as those built before the town charter, disappeared or metamorphosed into larger buildings a long time ago. Nevertheless, one can still get a glimpse of what most of the town might have looked like during its early development.

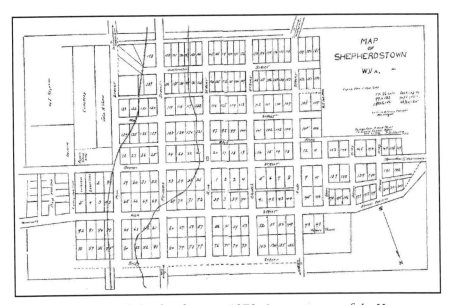

FIGURE 2.2 Map of Shepherdstown, 1873. *Image courtesy of the Historic Shepherdstown Commission.*

A few modest unclad log houses still stand west of Duke Street beyond the four-way stop at German Street. The lots where these houses stand were among those created by the Virginia Legislature in 1798. Therefore, these log houses are probably not from the earliest period of the town, However, they might be the first houses on their lots and appear— without measuring them—to conform to the minimum size required by the town charter.

There are undoubtedly other early log-constructed houses around town concealed behind clapboards, stucco, or brick. One can almost imagine the length of German Street and other streets around town dotted with buildings like the one in Figure 2.3. One can still catch glimpses through windows of exposed log walls inside buildings on German Street. The first brick dwellings began to supplant log houses about 1794, when Welsh's brick yard opened south of Washington Street, between Princess and King Streets.[34]

There may be misleading dates on some brick houses. Take a sizable brick house on German Street that bears a plaque with the year 1763. This year

may refer to an earlier home on the lot, which the current brick structure replaced. Or, if the existing house indeed dates from 1763, it may have received a brick-veneer outer layer long after its construction.

I found a real estate advertisement in the *Potomak Guardian and Berkeley Advertiser* of March 23, 1797, for a

FIGURE 2.3 Log house west of Duke Street. *Credit: Joseph Goss.*

400-acre farm one-and-a-half miles south of Shepherdstown, the exact distance to our log farmhouse. Abraham Morgan placed the ad. He was one of Colonel William Morgan's sons and his surviving executor. The advertisement for the farm described it containing "100-acres of cleared land under a good fence, two small houses, two barns, and a good well of water," belonging to Colonel Morgan's estate.[35]

I wondered if one of those houses could be ours. The ad bore no hint of whether any part of the advertised farm was on Colonel Morgan's 1756 land grant where our log farmhouse stands.

I searched the grantor and grantee deed records at the Berkeley County Historical Society, hoping to find a deed corresponding to the 1797 sale of the advertised farm. Such a deed could hold the earliest evidence connecting an owner with our log farmhouse if it was one of the two small houses mentioned in the advertisement. And if Walter B. Selby were the grantee of the sought deed, it would be a significant advance

---

34 Musser, 28.

35 Morgan, Abraham, "Advertisement for Sale of 400 Acre Farm," *Potomak Guardian and Berkeley Advertiser*, March 23, 1797, 3. BCHS microfilm archives.

in my research. I found no deed that matched the farm in the 1797 advertisement, putting an end to this tantalizing hope.

Eventually, I transcribed twenty-nine handwritten deeds in Berkeley and Jefferson Counties dating from 1797 to 1874 as part of this project—most of them naming Walter B. Selby as the grantee. These were the most likely deeds to reveal when and from whom he bought the log farmhouse and land. I summarize each of these deeds in Appendix A. In Chapter 5, we will see how these deeds and other evidence revealed what I sought.

Let me now introduce two wills, which I guessed could have a bearing on the provenance of our farmhouse. Captain Richard Morgan, Colonel William Morgan's father, died in 1763. His last will declared his plan to leave 400 acres of land to his son William for the use of William's eldest sons, Ralph, George, and Abraham. Keep George in mind for later. Richard Morgan had obtained this tract through a land grant on October 2, 1756. His 400-acre tract lay along the northern and eastern boundaries of Colonel William Morgan's September 14, 1756 land grant on which the farmhouse stands.[36]

I found no appraisal or settlement of Richard Morgan's estate, which might have described features like houses or other improvements on his 400-acre tract. His will offers no further clues about the earliest ownership of the log farmhouse. Nevertheless, Colonel William Morgan could have combined parts of his father's 400-acre tract with his adjoining 300-acre tract in a way that the log farmhouse could have stood on a parcel carved out of the two adjacent land grants. Colonel Morgan might then have allotted this hypothesized parcel to one of his three sons mentioned in Richard Morgan's will.

The other will I found was that of Colonel William Morgan himself. It is a noteworthy will, since it surfaces, transcribed from the handwritten original, on several websites including the Library of Virginia's. This recognition may reflect Colonel Morgan's stature in the early settlement of western Virginia and his distinguished military career spanning the French and Indian and Revolutionary Wars.

---

36 Bedinger Family History and Genealogy, "Last Will and Testament of Capt. Richard Morgan," November 14, 1763. Retrieved from http://www.bedinger.org/the-morgan -family.html

Colonel Morgan's last will was recorded at court in Berkeley County on October 21, 1788.[37] In it, he attests that he is "weak in body, but of sound memory blessed by God for his Mercies," in the pleasing standard testamentary language of that age. The will goes on to divide 1,554 acres among his seven children—Abraham, Zacheus, Rawleigh, Ralph, George, Sarah, and Elenor. Elenor, aka Eleanor, was Walter B. Selby's future wife. Colonel Morgan also left land to his grandsons, Abel and William, and his niece, Sarah O. Stogdon, daughter of his sister, Olive.

Sarah Stogdon's inherited land appears to have been in Kentucky, where Colonel Morgan had a connection. He took a party of adventurers to Kentucky in 1779, where his son Ralph settled.[38] Also, Colonel Morgan's will refers to a remainder tract of unspecified acreage, which his heirs were to sell to the highest bidder when its lease expired. This remainder tract turned out to be 569 ¾ acres, and its eventual sale yielded valuable details that allowed me not only to prove who was the original owner of our farmhouse but also to plot the boundaries of its farmland.

Although I could not make a direct link between Colonel Morgan's will and the log farmhouse, the will leaves 200-acre tracts to each of three sons—Zacheus, George, and Abraham—and says the parcels are those where each then lived in 1788. While not mentioned in the will, all three of these tracts must have included standing houses, suggesting that the log farmhouse could have belonged to one of these sons.

The will names Abraham and George as executors of Colonel Morgan's estate. The court did not appraise the estate until 1796 nor settle all its accounts until 1800.[39,40] The documents associated with these proceedings yielded a couple of interesting historical details. Part of the appraisal included four Negro slaves—Levi, Luce, Tom, and Sall—valued at a total of £277 10s. The complete account appraisal amounted to £927 18s. 9d. in Pennsylvania currency and £742 9s. in Virginia currency.

---

37 Morgan, Col. William, "Last Will and Testament," *Will Book 2*, Pages 5–8, September 9, 1788. BCHS microfilm archives.

38 Dandridge, 336.

39 Berkeley County Clerk, *Will Book 2*, Page 1, June 7, 1796.

40 Berkeley County Clerk, *Will Book 3*, Pages 288–291, March 9, 1800.

It seems that states issued currency in pounds sterling during all or part of the Revolutionary War, but did not standardize their values. Perhaps the court appraised Colonel Morgan's estate in out-of-date currency to capture its value more accurately since he got all of it before the end of the revolution. Why the court appraised his estate in both Pennsylvania and Virginia currencies is a puzzle I was unable to solve via internet research alone.

In the next chapter, we take a look at the strain of eighteenth- and nineteenth-century wars on life in Shepherdstown, especially the one cataclysmic war. We will also learn the roles played by some of the early owners of our farmhouse and a distinguished relative in those wars.

CHAPTER 3 WARS

THE HISTORICAL EXPERIENCE of greatest consequence to Shepherdstown, our farmhouse, and its land was undeniably war. The French and Indian War, the Revolutionary War, and the War with Mexico did not disturb Shepherdstown and the surrounding farms a great deal or at all. However, the Civil War had a shattering effect on Shepherdstown and its environs. The Battle of Antietam outside nearby Sharpsburg, Maryland, completely overwhelmed Shepherdstown and its neighboring farms. A depiction of the devastating repercussions of Antietam and the dauntless heroism of local people in its wake will follow consideration of the earlier wars.

French and Indian War

In 1755, Captain Richard Morgan raised a company in the vicinity of Shepherdstown to defend frontier settlements against Indian attacks. He acquired the title of Captain while serving the British cause in the French and Indian War, which spanned the years 1754 to 1763.[41,42,43] His son, William, served in his father's company, but we do not know what role he played. This era was a time when the Shepherdstown area had few inhabitants, and our log farmhouse undoubtedly did not exist. However, it was the time when William Morgan obtained the original land grant where the farmhouse stands.

The closest battles to Shepherdstown of this war were at Fort Cumberland, Maryland, Fort Necessity, Pennsylvania, and Fort Duquesne—present-day Pittsburgh. Shepherdstown was not in the path of either Colonel George Washington's troops or General Edward Braddock's troops to those battles. Washington marched through Pennsylvania to the north and Braddock through the southern tip of what is now Jefferson County. Local action in western Virginia typically involved Indian raids. British authorities in the west encouraged and supplied Indians to attack the French the same as the French did for them

---

41 Wood, Don C., "Springdale Farm, William Morgan House," undated. BCHS Morgan Family Files.

42 Wood, Don C., "Morgan Families of Old Berkeley," undated. BCHS Morgan Family Files.

43 Theriault, 19.

to attack the British. But often Indian raiding parties acted alone picking off isolated families and attacking small forts.[44]

One source tells that "unfriendly Indians drove citizens into the fort that once stood in the center of [Shepherds]town."[45] This fort might have occupied part of the site where McMurran Hall stands today. Captain Richard Morgan and his son, William, went with Colonel Adam Stephen of Martinsburg and a company of riflemen from Shepherdstown to join General Braddock at Fort Cumberland.[46] My point here is not to provide complete details of these events but only to provide a backdrop for the undertakings of some of our main characters during this war.

William Morgan received the following commission as Lieutenant during the French and Indian War:

> Francis Fauquier, Esq., His Majesty's Lieutenant Governor and Commander in Chief of the Colony and Dominion of Virginia: To William Morgan, Gent. By Virtue of His Majesty's Royal Commission and instructions appointing me Lieutenant Governor and Commander in Chief in and over his colony and Dominion of Virginia with full Power and Authority to appoint all officers both Civil and Military within the same. I, reposing especial Trust in your Loyalty, Courage, and good conduct do by these presents, appoint you, William Morgan, Lieutenant in a company of Militia of the County of Frederick Commanded by Van Swearingen Gent. You are therefore to act as your Cammand [sic], taking particular care that they be provided with Arms and Ammunition as the Laws of the Colony direct. And you are to observe and follow such Orders and directions from time and time, as you shall receive from me or any other of your superior officers, according to the rules and discipline of War in pursuance of the Trust reposed in you. Given at Williamsburg, under my hand and the seal of the Colony, this ninth day of November, and in the thirty second year of his Majesty's Reign, Annoque Domini 1758. Francis Fauquier.[47]

---

44 Sullivan, Ken, "The Revolutionary War," May 8, 2015. Retrieved from http://www.wvencyclopedia.org/articles/70

45 Milne, Kristin, "Thomas Shepherd's Town," *Mid-Atlantic Country*, September, 1990.

46 Bedinger Family History and Genealogy, "The Morgan Family." Retrieved from http://www.bedinger.org/the-morgan-family.html

47 Ancestry.com, "Descendants of David Janse Swierngh," 9–10, undated. Retrieved from http://freepages.genealogy.rootsweb.ancestry.com/~chafinmarsh/michener/descswearingen.pdf

I did not find out when William Morgan became a Colonel, but he held that rank at the beginning of the Revolutionary War. By then he had changed allegiance to support the rebellion.

Revolutionary War

There do not appear to have been any battles near Shepherdstown during the Revolutionary War period of 1775 to 1783. Nonetheless, western Virginians took part on both sides of the conflict and on battlefields throughout the country. Parallel frontier wars continued during the revolution like those of the French and Indian War.

In answer to a call by the Second Continental Congress in June 1775, Captain Hugh Stephenson enlisted ninety-eight riflemen in the vicinity of Shepherdstown. Their mission was to rush to reinforce General George Washington at his headquarters in Cambridge, Massachusetts. These were the first regular troops of the rebelling colonies. On July 17, the company rallied at Morgan's Spring—also called Stephenson's Spring—next to Colonel William Morgan's house, Springdale Farm, and Richard Morgan's small stone house at Falling Spring. Here the company began the famous Bee Line March, which took only twenty-five days to cover the 600 miles to Cambridge. By the war's end, seven companies had served from the Shepherdstown area, including 100 soldiers from the town.[48]

It is likely that, after leaving Morgan's Spring, Stephenson's company marched along part of an ancient stone wall, which still survives on one side of present-day Shepherdstown Pike near Engle Molers Road. This wall thus serves as a daily reminder to travelers of that long-ago march, and it stands less than three-quarters of a mile from the old farmhouse. The modern Bee Line Estates subdivision along Shepherdstown Pike also reminds motorists of the march.

After winning independence, it was time for the people to set about building the new nation. Benjamin Latrobe (1764–1820), the first Architect of the Capitol, was undoubtedly one of those builders. I came across a particularly interesting piece of his writing, which might have described conditions similar to those in the countryside around

---

48 Suttenfield, Diane, "Spirit of 1775 Beeline March to Cambridge," 2012, plaque located at King and German Streets, Shepherdstown, W.Va..

FRONTIER CABIN STORY

Shepherdstown. During his trips to the quarries where workers cut the stones for the U.S. Capitol building in Washington, Latrobe made observations of some of the living conditions along the route.

The quarries were forty-five miles south of Washington along the Potomac River at Aquia Creek. However, similar living conditions may have existed near Shepherdstown and other rural Virginia localities, but I hope not at our small farmhouse. The distressing circumstances Latrobe describes fly in the face of conventional beliefs about the industriousness and respectability of the area's German, English, Scottish, and Welsh settlers. The following extended quote—paragraph breaks added—is from Latrobe's journal entry entitled "A Rowdy Backcountry Household," dated August 23, 1806:

> In my trips to the quarries I have remarked upon the hundreds of half-starved, miserably lodged idled, besotted and ague and fever-smitten families, that inhabit the country of the Patowmack, and indeed I may say all the country of the slave states below the mountains. These people are either tenants to great landlords, or possess little farms themselves, or only inhabit miserable log houses and hire themselves occasionally as laborers. The river and creeks supply them most amply, in common seasons with shad and herrings at the expense of a little labor and salt. A few pigs and fowls are kept with scarcely any expense in the woods. The pigs give bacon.
>
> The little labor they do for themselves (and generally they cultivate a little land), gives them as much corn as supports them, and vegetables, that is cabbage, to their bacon, groceries, and the great source of their whiskey. To the wretched animals in the form of women with whom they cohabit, they are not always married. These beasts of burthen are absolutely slaves to their sottish husbands. They spin a little and make up household cloths, chiefly cotton, and also Lindsey, and earn a little whiskey by spinning for more decent wealthy families and neighbors.
>
> This tribe of wretched (I am told they are happy) families is numerous enough and their votes at an election are not unimportant. . . . [A friend said to Latrobe]: The ague and fever they don't mind it half as much as you do. . . . But the dripping of their huts, the open state of their log walls, which admit the winter's blast from every quarter, their wretched food, often scanty, never certain, their constant fighting and quarreling with each other. The beaten wives the horned husbands, the filthy diseases of poverty itch-scald heads.
>
> There is always some dry corner under their dripping roofs and if they get wet, whiskey keeps the cold out. Whiskey is better than a tight wall

against a northwestern gale. Whiskey is a substitute for all solid food. And an hour's labor earns a day's drunkenness, fighting is an amusement and all quarrels are made up over a glass of whiskey; beaten wives, find more than enough comfort in whiskey; and horned husbands, besides the whiskey, find pleasure in beating their wives.

As to itch and all these matters, they care less about than you do a mosquito bite. What can be said of all this? These dogs are independent of every human being; they are saucy, care not a damn for the best gentleman in the land, own no control, either of morals, manners, principles, law, and have no master but whiskey.[49]

The population that Latrobe and his friend wrote about were no doubt only a part of society, which also included the more distinguished figures portrayed in this narrative. Nevertheless, all must have lived side-by-side in a mutually advantageous compact. As my research progressed, I began to realize that the early occupants of our farmhouse were unlikely to have been the types Latrobe describes. I will explain my thinking on this subject in more detail when we get to the farm's tenants in Chapter 7.

War of 1812 and War with Mexico

The War of 1812 seems to have had no direct impact on Shepherdstown. However, in the run-up to the war, Shepherdstown leaders protested the restrictive trade policies of Presidents Thomas Jefferson and James Madison. On the other hand, restrictions on imports might have invigorated crafts production in the town.

Once the war started, Shepherdstown sent three companies to the conflict. Captain Henry Van Swearingen, a relative of Walter Selby's business partner, recruited a unit of riflemen. One writer tells of a Shepherdstown man, Michael Durnhoeffer, who jumped onto the wall of Fort George on the Niagara River in Upper Canada under a rain of cannonballs, took off his hat, and shouted "Hurrah for old Shepherdstown," when Americans took the fort. The same writer reported that it was mainly Shepherdstown men who resisted the British attack at another engagement—the Battle of Plattsburg, New York.[50]

49 Surkamp, James T., editor, "The Land Where We Were Dreamin', A People's History of Jefferson County, West Virginia," 2002, 32, Scarborough Library, Jefferson County Special Collection, Shepherd University.
50 Thomas, Jerry B., "War of 1812," Historic Shepherdstown & Museum. Retrieved from http://historicshepherdstown.com/portfolio-item/war-of-1812/

The War with Mexico fought between 1846 and 1848 happened far from Shepherdstown; however, local notable, Colonel John Francis Hamtramck, distinguished himself there. He also married two of Walter Selby's daughters—the second after the death of the first. I will present much more of his captivating story and personal papers in chapters to come.

Unlike these two wars, the Civil War had a devastating effect on Shepherdstown.

Civil War

Several Civil War battles affected Shepherdstown, such as Harpers Ferry and South Mountain. But I will focus only on the closer Battle of Antietam in Maryland and the Battle of Shepherdstown. The horrific Battle of Antietam, in which 23,000 soldiers perished, took place September 17 and 18, 1862.

FIGURE 3.1 Mary Bedinger Mitchell. *Image courtesy of Bedinger and Dandridge Family Papers, David M. Rubenstein Rare Book & Manuscript Library, Duke University.*

One very young girl living south of town wrote eyewitness observations of the residents of Shepherdstown and their experiences in the lead-up to and during the Battle of Antietam. She was then only eleven years old. This child was Mary Bedinger Mitchell (1850–1896), shown as an adult in Figure 3.1.[51]

Mary was the daughter of Henry Bedinger (1812–1858), elected to the U.S. Congress twice and appointed the first

---

51 Mitchell, Mary Bedinger, "A Woman's Recollection of Antietam," September 1862. Retrieved from http://www.bedinger.org/bios-and-sketches.html

Chargé d'Affaires to Denmark in 1853. Her younger sister was Carolina Danske Bedinger Dandridge (1854–1914), a chronicler of Shepherdstown history and a poet already noted in Chapter 2. The Bedingers were early settlers in Shepherdstown and related to the Morgan family by marriage.

The Bedinger family home, Rosebrake, was a little south of Shepherdstown. Hence, the effects of Antietam at our farmhouse further to the east must have been comparable to some of those described by Mitchell. Although Mitchell was writing about her own experiences, I think they were familiar to most people in and near the town. Mitchell's writing, of course, reflects her Virginia upbringing and sympathy for the cause of the Confederacy.

Her remarkable account entitled "A Woman's Recollections of Antietam," first appeared in 1866 in *Century Magazine* under the pseudonym of Mary Blunt. The article came out later in the book *Battles and Leaders of the Civil War*, a collection of stories and essays edited by Johnson and Buel, published in 1877.[52] By this time Mitchell and her editors had set down her account in a more mature voice than that of a child eyewitness.

I chose to use extended excerpts from Mitchell's article because they bring the writer's voice and her experiences to life much more colorfully than paraphrasing could. Mitchell writes:

> In this odd little borough, then, we were waiting 'developments,' hearing first that 'our men were coming,' and then that they were not coming, when suddenly, . . . early in the morning, we found ourselves surrounded by a hungry horde of lean and dusty tatterdemalions. . . . They were stragglers . . . worn out by the incessant strain of that summer.[53]

> When I say that they were hungry, I convey no impression of the gaunt starvation that looked from their cavernous eyes. All day they crowded to the doors of our houses, with always the same drawling complaint: 'I've been a-marchin' an' a-fightin' for six weeks stiddy; and I ain't had n-a-r-thin' to eat 'cept green apples an' green cawn, an' I wish you'd please to gimme a bite to eat.'. . . There was little mitigation of hardship to our unfortunate armies. We were fond of calling them Spartans, and they were but too truly called upon to endure a Spartan system of neglect and privation. They were always ill-fed and ill-cared for. . . .

---

52 Mitchell.
53 From the fighting at Harpers Ferry.

[T]he approaching wounded . . . here they were, unannounced, on the brick pavements, and the first thing was to find roofs to cover them.

Men ran for keys and opened the long empty shops and unused rooms; other people got brooms and stirred up the dust of ages; then armies of children began to appear with bundles of hay and straw, taken from anybody's stable. These were hastily disposed in heaps, and covered with blankets—the soldiers' own, or else one begged or borrowed from anywhere. On these improvised beds the sufferers were placed, and the next question was of the proper dressing of their wounds. No surgeons were to be seen. . . .

Our women set bravely to work and washed away the blood, or stanched it as well as they could, where the jolting of the long, rough ride had disarranged the hasty binding done upon the battle-field. But what did they know of wounds beyond a cut finger, or a boil? Yet they bandaged and bathed, with a devotion that went far to make up for their inexperience. . . . On our side of the river there were noise, confusion, dust; throngs of stragglers; horsemen galloping about; wagons blocking each other and teamsters wrangling, and a continued din of shouting swearing, and rumbling, in the midst of which men were dying, fresh wounded arriving, surgeons amputating limbs and dressing wounds, women going in and out with bandages, lint, medicines, food. An ever-present sense of anguish, dread, pity, and, I fear, hatred—these are my recollections of Antietam. . . . The wounded continued to arrive until the town was quite unable to hold all the disabled and suffering.

They filled every building and overflowed into the country round, into farmhouses, barns, corn-cribs, cabins—wherever four walls and a roof were found together. There were six churches and they were all full; the Odd Fellows' Hall, the Free Masons, the little town council room, the barn-like place known as the Drill Room, all the private houses after their capacity, the shops and empty buildings, the school-houses—every inch of space, and yet the cry was for more room.

Mitchell's reference to the overflowing of wounded soldiers into farmhouses in the countryside near Shepherdstown inevitably would have included our farmhouse, although there is no record or visible sign of this today. As I will tell later, at least I have clues about who lived at the farmhouse at this time. While I have omitted part of her narrative here, Mitchell continues:

[I]n the morning we found the Confederate army in full retreat. General Lee crossed the Potomac under cover of the darkness, and when the day broke the greater part of his force or the more orderly portion of it— had gone on towards Kearneysville and Leetown.

The better people kept some outward coolness, with perhaps a sort of 'noblesse oblige' feeling but the poorer classes acted as if the town were already in a blaze, and rushed from their houses with their families and household goods to make their way into the country. The road was thronged, the streets blocked; men were vociferating, women crying, children screaming; wagons, ambulances, guns, caissons, horsemen, footmen, all mingled—nay, even wedged and jammed together—in one struggling, shouting mass. It was Pandemonium. The Negroes were the worst, and with faces of a ghastly ash color, they swarmed into the fields, carrying their babies, their clothes, their pots and kettles, fleeing from the wrath behind them. . . . Those maimed and bleeding fugitives! When the firing commenced the hospitals began to empty. All who were able to pull one foot after another, or could bribe or beg comrades to carry them, left in haste.

In vain we implored them to stay; in vain we showed them the folly, the suicide, of the attempt; in vain we argued, cajoled, threatened, ridiculed; pointed out that we were remaining and that there was less danger here than on the road.

There is no sense or reason in a panic. . . . [M]en with arms in slings, without arms, with one leg, with bandaged sides and backs; men in ambulances, wagons, carts, wheelbarrows, men carried on stretchers, or supported on the shoulder of some self-denying comrade—all who could crawl went, and went to almost certain death.

They could not go far, they dropped off into the country houses, where they were received with as much kindness as it was possible to ask for; but their wounds had become inflamed and angry, their frames were weakened by fright and over-exertion; erysipelas, mortification, gangrene set in; and the long rows of nameless graves still bear witness to the results.

Although I believe our farmhouse must have sheltered wounded from the Battle of Antietam, as already mentioned, we have not found any Civil War artifacts on the property. We hoped we might see some from the excavation for a substantial addition to the house in 2013, but we did not. An acquaintance has surveyed parts of the property with a metal detector but found nothing. Still, this does not rule out the possibility that someone noticed and removed artifacts from the property before our ownership. Today the farmhouse property encompasses only about four percent of the 245 acres it included as recently as 2001 leaving open the possibility that artifacts may exist on the former farmhouse property beyond its current boundaries making them difficult to find or access. Construction of the Wrights Field subdivision on much of the old farm property could have displaced or eradicated any artifacts that might have fallen there.

The two-day Battle of Shepherdstown took place September 19 and 20, 1862, in the aftermath of Antietam. It ended in a stalemate with troops staring at each other across the Potomac. Nonetheless, it was the war's bloodiest engagement in the region soon to become West Virginia. Seventy-three Union soldiers and thirty-six Confederate soldiers died in the battle, and the injured numbered many more. One Union soldier described Shepherdstown as not much of an encounter as modern battles go, but it had significant consequences.

The sketch in Figure 3.2 by Alfred R. Waud, an artist for *Harper's Weekly* and an eyewitness to the Battle of Shepherdstown, depicts some Union soldiers resting and others firing across the Potomac River from Maryland at their Confederate counterparts. By some chance, J. P. Morgan gave this sketch to the Library of Congress in 1919.[54] Was he aware of the Morgans of Shepherdstown?

FIGURE 3.2 Battle of Shepherdstown.
Image courtesy of Library of Congress, Morgan Collection of Civil War Drawings, Prints & Photographs Division.

The Battle of Shepherdstown marked the end of Confederate General Robert E. Lee's first invasion of the North, which Union soldiers effectively repulsed at Antietam. Also, the Battle of Shepherdstown, where Lee's army retreated into Virginia, convinced Union General George B. McClellan that a second invasion was possible. This assessment paralyzed the Union Army in Maryland for the next

---

54 Waud, Alfred R., "Ford near Shepherdstown, on the Potomac. Pickets firing across the river," Library of Congress. Retrieved from http://www.loc.gov/pictures /item/2004660886/

month giving Lee's army time to regroup. In consequence, President Abraham Lincoln removed McClellan out of disgust for his lack of potency.[55]

This battle took place extremely close to our farmhouse. A historical marker at the corner of Engle Molers and Trough Roads memorializes it. A map of troop movements during the battle appears in Figure 3.3. It shows that some of the action might have taken place on our farmhouse's current ten-acre property.[56] Thus it is even more disappointing that we have found no military artifacts.

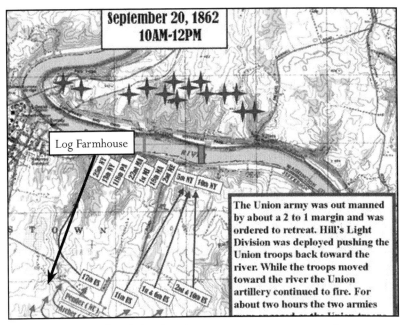

FIGURE 3.3 Battle of Shepherdstown troop movements. *Image courtesy of Shepherdstown Battlefield Preservation Association.*

Although it occurred during the midst of the Civil War, how West Virginia achieved its secession from Virginia and rejoined the Union is a separate and quite interesting matter of its own.

---

55 Noyalas, Jonathan A., "Battle of Shepherdstown," *Encyclopedia Virginia*, April 30, 2012. Retrieved from http://www.EncyclopediaVirginia.org/Shepherdstown_Battle_of

56 Shepherdstown Battlefield Preservation Association Inc., "The 1862 Battle of Shepherdstown," undated. Retrieved from http://shepherdstownbattlefield .org/1862battlemaps/

Statehood

At the start of the Civil War, the northwestern counties of Virginia, excluding the Eastern Panhandle, overwhelmingly opposed the state's secession from the Union declared on April 17, 1861. Powerless to halt their state's withdrawal, western Virginians quickly took advantage of a long-awaited opening for their own separation from Virginia. One of the reasons behind this movement was the considerable difference in wealth between Tidewater and Piedmont Virginia and the western part of the state. The resulting political neglect and disempowerment of the west, as well as clear class differences, drove many inhabitants to believe that Richmond did not pay adequate attention to their interests.

Shielded by Union troops, representatives from most of Virginia's western counties met at Wheeling on June 11, 1861, and annulled the Virginia secession ordinance. They proclaimed the offices of the government at Richmond vacated, and formed the restored government of Virginia, under the governorship of Francis H. Pierpont. A referendum held on October 24, 1861, approved creation of this new political entity briefly named the State of Kanawha after a major river in the southwestern part of the new state. Within six months a constitutional convention changed the name to West Virginia to convey the representatives' longing to reflect their Virginia heritage and to avoid the new state being confused with Kanawha County.

In November 1861, another convention at Wheeling drafted a state constitution and approved it in April 1862. President Lincoln decreed admission of West Virginia to the United States effective on June 20, 1863. Arthur I. Boreman became its first governor. Francis H. Pierpont's restored government of Virginia, of course, had consented to the establishment of the new state, thereby fulfilling the U.S. constitutional requirement that a state had to agree to its own division.[57]

A highly controversial decision concerning the formation of West Virginia involved the Eastern Panhandle counties, which supported the

---

57 Family Education Network, infoplease, "West Virginia History, Civil War and the Creation of West Virginia." Retrieved from https://www.infoplease.com/encyclopedia /places/united-states-canada-and-greenland/us-political-geography/west-virginia/history

Confederacy and did not initially enter into the new state. The federal government ordered an election in 1863 to allow the residents of Jefferson and Berkeley counties to decide whether they ought to be in Virginia or West Virginia. Union troops stood guard outside polling places to give pause to residents who might vote for Virginia. These guards appear to have had the desired effect. Despite local support for Virginia, residents who filled out ballots voted overwhelmingly to place both counties in West Virginia. The Baltimore and Ohio Railroad, which ran through the Eastern Panhandle, was crucial to Union troop movements and the northern economy. Placing these counties in West Virginia put the entire railroad beyond the reach of the Confederacy.[58]

I will begin to piece together the puzzle of who first owned and lived in our farmhouse in the next couple of chapters. To do this we will need to turn the clock back more than a century before the Civil War when the thirteen colonies were still under British rule, West Virginia was not yet a state, and our log house not yet built.

58 "West Virginia Statehood," West Virginia Archives and History, 2018. Retrieved from http://www.wvculture.org/history/archives/statehoo.html

CHAPTER 4 EARLIEST OWNERS

W E WILL NOW turn to the people who had an early connection to the log farmhouse or its land. I mentioned previously that Thomas Fairfax (1693–1781) claimed the entire Northern Neck of Virginia. King Charles II first contrived the Northern Neck Proprietary, or Fairfax Grant, while in exile in 1649. The grant became effective in 1660 when Charles returned to the throne. Thomas Culpeper (1635–1689) acquired all rights to the land from Charles II in 1681.[59]

Thomas Fairfax

Thomas Culpeper was Thomas Fairfax's maternal grandfather. Through inheritance, Thomas Fairfax claimed all 5,282,000 acres of the Northern Neck Proprietary. The master of Leeds Castle at Oxford, his lordship did not fully enjoy the privileges of the English nobility because his father had squandered much of the family fortune.[60] In London, Thomas Fairfax had been a member of a literary society. He was a friend of Joseph Addison and contributed to Addison's daily, *The Spectator*, which promoted marriage, family, and courtesy. It appears that Thomas Fairfax retired from society due to a disappointment in love—his fiancée married another man.[61] So much for marriage and family for Fairfax, whose portrait appears in Figure 4.1.[62]

I was not familiar with either Joseph Addison or *The Spectator*. Therefore, it surprised me to find in my personal reading while working on this project that Addison inspired writer and Nobel Laureate, John Steinbeck. He even quotes the 1711 first issue of *The Spectator* in his *Travels with Charley, In Search of America* in connection with his desire to emulate

---

59 Wikipedia contributors, "Thomas Fairfax, 6th Lord Fairfax of Cameron." Retrieved from https://en.wikipedia.org/wiki/Thomas_Fairfax,_6th_Lord_Fairfax_of_Cameron

60 Brown, Stuart E. Jr., "Virginia Baron: The Story of Thomas 6th Lord Fairfax." Retrieved from http://www.genealogical.com/index.php?main_page=productinfo&item _number=9798

61 Browne, Allen C., "Landmarks, Greenway Court." Retrieved from http://allenbrowne .blogspot.com/2012/05/greenway-court.html

62 Horydczak, Theodor, photographer, "Lord Fairfax VI, Masonic Lodge, Alexandria I," Library of Congress. Retrieved from http://www.loc.gov/pictures/item /thc1995011945/PP/

Addison's conviction that a reader should have a "right understanding of an author."[63] This finding is an example of how my research could have continued indefinitely or until my curiosity ran out. I say this hoping to give the reader a right understanding of this book's author and to defend the many departures I took from my professed goals of learning who first owned or built our farmhouse and its year of construction.

FIGURE 4.1 Thomas Fairfax. *Image courtesy Library of Congress Prints and Photographs Division.*

Struggling to support an expensive lifestyle at Leeds Castle, Fairfax relied on the income from the sale of land grants from his Virginia territory and the annual ground rents paid by the grantees. His land agent, Robert "King" Carter (1662–1732), collected these proceeds.

In the fall of 1732, Fairfax read Carter's obituary in the London monthly, *The Gentleman's Magazine,* and learned of the vast personal wealth Carter had accumulated. It amounted to £10,000 in cash at a time when the governor of Virginia received an annual salary of £200. Instead of appointing another Virginian to the position, Thomas Fairfax had his cousin, Colonel William Fairfax (1691–1757), move from Massachusetts to Virginia in 1734 to serve as his resident land agent.

Thomas Fairfax traveled to Virginia for the first time between 1735 and 1737 to inspect and protect his lands. Returning to America in 1747, he first settled at Fort Belvoir, an estate completed by Colonel William Fairfax in 1741. He became personally active in developing his lands

---

63 Steinbeck, John, *Travels with Charley, In Search of America*, originally published: New York: Viking Press, 1962; Penguin Books, 1986, 38–39.

and collecting ground rents. Thomas Fairfax was the only permanent resident peer in North America, and although other peers held offices in the colonies, they later returned to England. In 1748, he met George Washington—a distant relative of the Yorkshire Fairfax family—who was then only sixteen. Impressed with Washington's energy and talents, Thomas Fairfax granted Washington his first employment to survey his lands lying west of the Blue Ridge Mountains.

Thomas Fairfax moved out to the Shenandoah Valley in 1752. At the suggestion of his nephew and City of Martinsburg's namesake, Thomas Bryan Martin, he fixed his residence at a hunting lodge at Greenway Court, south of Winchester. There Fairfax and Martin lived in a style of generous hospitality, often indulging in the hunt. He served as lieutenant and Justice of the Peace for Frederick County. Although he had no direct heirs, the Fairfax line continues with Nicholas John Albert Fairfax, the fourteenth Lord Fairfax of Cameron (b. 1956), who lives in England.[64]

Though Fairfax was an avowed loyalist, the separatists never molested him. The legislature, however, confiscated his lands during the revolution by the Virginia Acts of 1779. Less than two months after the 1781 defeat of General Cornwallis at Yorktown, the eighty-eight-year-old Thomas Fairfax died at Greenway Court.[65]

Before its confiscation in 1779, the Northern Neck Proprietary was subject to prolonged and rancorous litigation, first between the grantees and the British Crown and later involving the Colony of Virginia and those who settled the lands. Besides, the illegitimate heirs of Thomas Culpeper's estate challenged its passing to Culpeper's only acknowledged child, Catherine—Thomas Fairfax's mother—and her husband, the fifth Lord Fairfax.[66]

Colonel William Morgan

I noted previously that, in 1756, Colonel William Morgan became the owner of the 300-acre land grant where builders eventually constructed

---

64 Wikipedia contributors, "Nicholas Fairfax, 14th Lord Fairfax of Cameron." Retrieved from https://en.wikipedia.org/w/index.php?title=Nicholas_Fairfax,_14th_Lord _Fairfax_of_Cameron&oldid=662954300

65 Wikipedia contributors, "Thomas Fairfax, 6th Lord Fairfax of Cameron."

66 HistoricHampshire.org, "Historic Hampshire County, Searching for Hampshire's English Roots." Retrieved from http://www.historichampshire.org/fairfax.htm

our log farmhouse. He and his father, Captain Richard Morgan, obtained many other land grants near Shepherdstown and far beyond, becoming two of the largest landowners in the vicinity. I found no evidence, however, that Colonel Morgan ever built a house on this 300-acre tract. Nonetheless, he did build for himself a stone house circa 1760, called Springdale Farm located out of view on the west side of Shepherdstown Pike near Engle Molers Road.[67] Sometime before the end of Colonel Morgan's life he moved to a house on Lot No. 65 in Shepherdstown. This is where he says he lived when he wrote his will in 1788.[68] Shepherd University now owns Lot No. 65, and the house is gone.

The "Reconstructed Census 1774–1810 of Berkeley County, Virginia," lists Colonel Morgan's household with three whites, four slaves, ten horses, and seventeen cattle for the year 1783. These facts speak of a prosperous person of that time. He was sixty years old in 1783 and still living at Springdale Farm judging from the size of his household. The reconstructed census did not list him during any other year.

Colonel Morgan's 1756 land grant has some fascinating provisions and language. The grant included all rights and appurtenances belonging to the land, except for royal mines and a third part of all lead, copper, tin, coal, iron mines, and ore, which might be on it. Colonel Morgan was to pay one shilling in annual ground rent for every fifty acres on the feast day of St. Michael the Arch Angel. If Colonel Morgan did not pay the rent for two whole years, Thomas Fairfax could repossess the land as if it were never granted. Thomas Fairfax prefaced his signature to the grant with the following words:

> Given at my office . . . under my hand and seal . . . in the thirtieth year of the Reign of our Sovereign Lord George the Second by the grace of God of Great Britain, France and Ireland King, Defender of the Faith, etc.[69]

Curious about King George II being "King of France," I checked to what extent England still held parts of France in 1756. Although the kings of England held extensive territories in France during the Middle Ages, by 1453 only the Pale of Calais—captured in 1347 and lost in 1558—was

---

67 Wood, Don C., "Morgan Families of Old Berkeley," written communication, undated. BCHS Morgan Family Files.

68 Morgan.

69 Northern Neck Grants.

still theirs. Today only the Channel Islands preserve their link to the British Crown.[70] Thus, the use of "King of France" in George II's title was a vestigial formality recalling long-lost territory and claims—arguably legitimate to some—to the French monarchy. King George III dropped it from his title at the beginning of the nineteenth century.[71]

There were at least five Morgan family lines having no immediate bond of relationship that settled in West Virginia. The best known was that of Colonel Morgan Morgan (1688–1766), the first European settler of the state, who settled at Bunker Hill in present-day Berkeley County in 1730 or 1731. Another Morgan family line was that of Captain Richard Morgan already introduced in previous chapters. He settled near Shepherdstown sometime between 1731 and 1734. The other Morgan lines arrived later and established themselves in other parts of the state.

The broader Morgan clan has imparted its name to Morgan County and Morgantown, West Virginia, the Morgan Horse, and the investment banking firms of Morgan Stanley and JP Morgan Chase, and includes nineteenth-century financier J. Pierpont Morgan. The Morgan family tree goes back as far as 1089 in Wales.[72,73] Morgan is a Welsh name meaning "born of the sea" or "son of the sea." The Morgan name played a part in the classic lore of the Knights of the Round Table. An archaic William Morgan, a common ancestor of the Morgans who came to America, according to legend translated the Bible into Welsh. King Morgan headed a line of Welsh kings and princes and was the founder of Glamorgan, Wales, and the family of Morgan.[74] I found no dates for any of these ancient figures.

Captain Richard Morgan (1690–1763) might have come from Wales but grew up in New Jersey according to the Welsh Valley Preservation Society. He could have arrived in Virginia with Joist Hite's group in 1731

70 Wikipedia contributors, "English overseas possessions." Retrieved from https://en.wikipedia.org/w/index.php?title=English_overseas_possessions&oldid=679144690

71 Wikipedia contributors, "English claims to the French throne." Retrieved from https://en.wikipedia.org/wiki/English_claims_to_the_French_throne

72 Morgan, French, *A History and Genealogy of the Family of Colonel Morgan Morgan, The First White Settler of the State of West Virginia (Preface)*, 1966, McClain Printing Co., Parsons, West Virginia.

73 Morgan Family Genealogy, "Genealogy." Retrieved from http://hausegenealogy.com/morgan.html

74 Name of Morgan - Reference 929.9, 7. BCHS Morgan Family Files.

or with those who followed over the next few years. He became quite prosperous and acquired several thousand acres near Shepherdstown and beyond. Richard Morgan married Jane Taylor (circa 1695–unk.) around 1710, and they had four sons and three daughters. In 1754, their eldest son, William David Morgan (1723–1788), married Drusilla Swearingen (1737–unk.), daughter of Thomas Swearingen.[75]

The name Richard Morgan surfaces a few times in other records, and I relate them here. In 1738, Thomas Shepherd petitioned the Orange County Court to discharge him as Constable Sherundo as soon as the court could swear Richard Morgan in to replace him. Sherundo, possibly a Native American term, was another name for Shenandoah. The same year, Shepherd collected a bounty of fourteen shillings for a wolf's head under Richard Morgan's direction—no doubt in his role as Constable Sherundo.[76]

George Morgan

Next, we turn to George Morgan (1752–1796), son of Colonel William Morgan, for reasons I will explain shortly. He married Drusilla Swearingen (1764–unk.), a first cousin with the same first and family names as his mother. They had at least four children—William, Raleigh (aka Rawleigh Jr.), Van, and Lydia.[77] In 1798, George Morgan's widow married Azariah Thornburg who died in 1807.[78] Twice widowed, Drusilla married Charles Williams in 1815.[79] One author relates that George Morgan became the U.S. Indian agent for the Middle Department headquartered at Pittsburgh in 1776.[80] After further research, I noticed that Indian agent George Morgan's years (1743–1810) did not match William Morgan's son George's years. Besides, Indian agent George Morgan was from Prospect,

---

75 Welsh Valley Preservation Society (WVPS), "Morgan Family Focus," *Valley Views, Quarterly Newsletter of the WVPS*, summer, 1987. BCHS Morgan Family Files.

76 National Conservation Training Center, "Early European Settlement of Terrapin Neck," Retrieved from https://training.fws.gov/history/virtualexhibits/nctcculturalhistory /Timeline1730.html

77 Lindley, Les, "History of Lindley, Councilman, and Associated Families." Retrieved from http://woodlin.net/lindley/4413.htm

78 Marriage records, West Virginia Department of Arts, Culture and History. Retrieved from http://www.wvculture.org/vrr/va_view.aspx?Id=12501451&Type=Marriage

79 Keesecker, Guy L., 159.

80 Smyth, 170.

New Jersey.[81] The *geni.com* website also mistakes Shepherdstown's George Morgan for the Indian agent of the same name. Indian agent George Morgan could still have been part of Captain Richard Morgan's family line since they both came from New Jersey, but he was not our George Morgan.

I was disappointed that Shepherdstown's George Morgan was not the George Morgan who made history by courageously writing to Williamsburg in 1777. His letter denounced the executive council of Virginia's resolution to make war upon a band of Indians that had besieged Fort Henry at Wheeling. He was contemptuous of any expedition into Indian country, which "involves us in a general and unequal Quarrel with all the nations who are at present quiet but extremely Jealous of the least encroachment on their lands." The executive council rescinded the original war resolution.[82] The Delawares so highly respected Indian agent Morgan for his justice and integrity that they universally called him "Tamanend," after their most famous chief.[83]

Judging from this case of mistaken identity, I believe there is much confused genealogical information on the internet concerning people who lived centuries ago. This problem may be due to overzealous but misinformed contributors and reuse of the same given names across multiple generations and different branches of a family. When researching accounts of historical figures with similar or the same names, one must thoroughly cross-check birth and death years, associated event dates, and birthplaces to avoid propagating demonstrably incorrect information. One must check several different sources when encountering confusing or questionable names and information while doing this type of research.

Danske Dandridge writes that George Morgan of Shepherdstown trekked the already noted Bee Line March to Cambridge, a significant deed, which set the colonies on a course to the birth of our country.[84] I found other remnants of George Morgan's life in the "Berkeley County Land Books of

81 Downes, Randolph C., "George Morgan, Indian Agent Extraordinary, 1776–1779," *Pennsylvania History: A Journal of Mid-Atlantic Studies*, Vol. 1, No. 1, Penn State University Press, October 1934, 203.
82 Smyth, 182.
83 Geni.com, "Colonel George Morgan's Geni Profile." Retrieved from http://www.geni.com/people/Col-George-Morgan/6000000003345334644
84 Dandridge, 176.

1782–1803." The land books listed him owning one lot and receiving rent in 1787, but do not record the acreage, its assessed value, or its location. He appears again in 1789 in the land books with his brother, Abraham. They owned land together according to the books, which give its assessed value but no acreage or location.

The only other fact I found about George Morgan was that he received 200 acres and a house in his father's 1788 will. He made no recorded will of his own, leaving in question to whom he left his home and land upon his death. By reading the deeds that documented the land's sale years after George Morgan's death, I learned that his children received his property. Why his widow, Drusilla, did not receive the property is not recorded. Perhaps it was due to her remarriages.

Two contemporary Morgan descendants who I will introduce shortly— George Alwin and Mary Ann Morgan—knew no more about the lives of Captain Richard or Colonel William Morgan than I have written in this narrative. They had never heard of George Morgan. They did not know of any personal papers or effects of the earliest Morgan generations, which might have come down through their families to the present. Nonetheless, George Alwin mentioned that an elderly relative owned an original hand-drawn plan of Shepherdstown drafted when people were beginning to lay out the town's lots.

He suggested that this plan predated any of the other historical lot maps in the public domain and that he hoped to inherit it eventually. I have not seen this document and cannot attest to its age or whether or not it is one of those already in the public domain. However, the suggestion of an undiscovered document gives me hope that others may be out there, which could surface in the future to help us better understand the lives of the people who settled Shepherdstown.

I found a plaque at the Old English Episcopal Cemetery on Church Street stating that Colonel William Morgan's remains lay beneath the chancel in the adjoining 1769 stone church building—the first Episcopal Church in Shepherdstown. This privileged burial place was in honor of his service in the French and Indian and Revolutionary Wars. I searched the same cemetery for George Morgan's grave, but could not find it.

I checked with the present Episcopal Church office on German Street to see if it had records of burials as far back as 1796, the year of George Morgan's death. Unfortunately, it only had records back to the mid-1800's. By chance, I found a listing of headstone inscriptions for Jefferson County cemeteries on the internet.[85] It lists only thirty-three names for the Old English Episcopal Cemetery, because, as the contributor states, most of the inscriptions were indecipherable due to their age. Although there are several Morgan headstones listed, George Morgan's is not among them. I spotted the website contributor—Anne Braun—when she was taking care of the cemetery grounds one evening. She mentioned to me that besides being indecipherable, some of the headstones lie face down or have even sunk below ground.[86]

Surviving Morgan Houses

Together with Captain Richard and Colonel William Morgan's homes at Falling Spring and Springdale Farm, George's, Abraham's, and Zacheus's homes and their 200-acre farms were part of a Morgan family settlement of side-by-side plantations. Colonel Morgan also gave 400 acres to three other children in his 1788 will—Ralph, who later settled in Kentucky, Rawleigh, and Sarah—which formed part of this eighteenth-century community. All these lands and home places adjoined each other shaping an immense Morgan family compound, now vanished, southeast of town.[87] Daughter Eleanor received the house on Lot No. 65 and its attached four-acre pasture. Since she was only six years old, rents from these properties paid for her schooling and necessities until she turned eighteen.[88]

At one point, Rawleigh owned the Wynkoop Tavern in town but sold it to Walter B. Selby in 1810, which I will comment on shortly. Rawleigh could still have owned another farm and house—perhaps ours—outside of town either before or during his ownership of the tavern. It is conceivable that our home stands on land he received in his father's will.

---

85 Interment.net, Anne Braun, contributor, "Trinity Episcopal Cemetery Jefferson County, West Virginia," April 7, 2003. Retrieved from http://www.interment.net/data/us/wv/jefferson/trinity/index.htm

86 Braun, Anne, personal communication, July 27, 2017.

87 Wood, Don C., "Springdale Farm William Morgan House," undated. BCHS Morgan Family Files.

88 Morgan.

The two Morgan descendants I have already mentioned, George Alwin and Mary Ann Morgan, still live in the Shepherdstown area. George Alwin, whom I met in person, is a fifth-generation descendant of Colonel William Morgan's nephew, Jacob Morgan—George Morgan's cousin. Mary Ann Morgan is the widow of another descendant of the same Jacob Morgan.

A note about Jacob Morgan's son, William, is in order. Colonel William Augustine Morgan (1831–1899) served in the Confederate Army during the Civil War. He is sometimes confused with his great-uncle, Colonel William David Morgan, the original owner of the land grant our farmhouse stands on.[89] I mention this to prevent others from mistaking one of these William Morgans for the other.

George Alwin and Mary Ann Morgan informed me that Richard Morgan's old stone house (circa 1734) at Falling Spring still stands and is occupied. It might be one of the three or four oldest dwellings in West Virginia. It is out of public view, but visible on satellite maps.

George Alwin also mentioned that Richard Morgan built an earlier weatherboard house on High Street in Shepherdstown.[90] This house appears to have survived until at least 1933 based on an archival photograph presented in Figure 4.2.[91] It is gone now—removed to make room for a newer dwelling. It must have been a few years older than Richard's 1734 stone house at Falling Spring, making it the oldest building in Shepherdstown with photographic evidence of its existence.

The weatherboard house cannot date from before the 1730's, as Richard Morgan settled in Shepherdstown in the early 1730's. Still, the photograph's caption dated it from 1727 when I first retrieved it from the Library of Congress's website. If true, this would have made it the oldest known abode in all of West Virginia. Even though I have mentioned the possibility of very early settlers in Chapter 2, most evidence I have found and cited previously suggests that 1727 is too early for any recorded Europeans to have settled in West Virginia. When I returned to the same

---

89 Bedinger Family History and Genealogy, "Colonel William Augustine Morgan." Retrieved from http://www.bedinger.org/colonel-william-a-morgan.html
90 Alwin, George, personal communication, July 11, 2017.
91 Historic American Buildings Survey, creator, "Richard Morgan House, High Street, Shepherdstown, Jefferson County, West Virginia," 1933, Library of Congress. Retrieved from https://www.loc.gov/item/wv0073/

website after several years, the photograph's caption did not indicate any date for the house. This change might reflect the correction of an error.

Mary Ann Morgan told me that Richard Morgan sold Thomas Shepherd some land where he founded his town. Another source confirmed this. It states that Richard Morgan sold Thomas Shepherd the fifty acres of land where much of present-day Shepherdstown lies.[92] However, the land-grant map of Jefferson County noted in Chapter 1 shows that most of the town stands on Shepherd's 222-acre land patent, which he had obtained for it. The map shows that Richard Morgan had procured a 1756 land grant of 155 acres, mainly east of Mill Street. The fifty-acre tract that Richard

FIGURE 4.2 Richard Morgan house.
Image courtesy of Library of Congress, Prints & Photographs Division, HABS.

Morgan sold to Thomas Shepherd must have been part of this land grant, which encompasses only a small part of the present-day town.

To my knowledge, there are only five houses likely built by Morgans in the eighteenth and early nineteenth centuries still standing near Shepherdstown. In chronological order, these are Captain Richard Morgan's stone house at Falling Spring (1734) and his son Colonel William Morgan's stone house at Springdale Farm (circa 1760). Next in line is our house (circa 1780), if we can infer that it was a Morgan house because of the 1756 land grant on which it stands. Colonel Morgan's nephew Daniel Morgan's residence (1803), later named Roscbrake, is next in order.

---

92 Historic Shepherdstown & Museum, "Family Histories Presented at Shepherdstown 250th Anniversary Coming Home Parade." Retrieved from http://historicshepherdstown .com/research/shepherdstown-250-parade/

Richard Morgan built Rosebrake's antecedent as a single-story settlement house about 1745. His grandson, Daniel Morgan, expanded it beginning in 1803 when he acquired it. Its name was Poplar Grove in 1859 when Danske Bedinger Dandridge's mother bought it. She changed its name to Rosebrake in 1877.[93] Finally, there is Daniel Morgan's brother Jacob Morgan's house, Falling Spring (1837), fittingly called "The Mansion" by the Morgan family descendants I contacted. This house is adjacent to Richard Morgan's stone house at Falling Spring. Lynne and I toured Falling Spring on April 29, 2017. Besides our own home, it is the only other early Morgan house that we have seen personally. Morgan family members do not occupy any of these houses today. If other old Morgan houses still survive near Shepherdstown, I have not heard of them.

Mary Ann Morgan told me that the Morgans lost their considerable wealth in consequence of the Civil War.[94] However, not all their old houses, if any, fell into other hands at that time. Our house passed out of the family in 1811. I will offer more details about this sale shortly. Further, a Morgan descendant still occupied Jacob Morgan's Falling Spring until 1904.

Before launching wholeheartedly into the Selby and Hamtramck families in the next two chapters, I want to help avert the inevitable confusion among names of members of these families as well as the Morgan family. I have developed two family trees in Appendix C to keep track of these personalities. Additionally, I have included individuals' familiar names besides their proper names to help achieve this.

In the next chapter, we will consider the absentee farmhouse landlords who offer the only available source of information to trace the log house's custody back to its original owner.

---

93 National Park Service, "National Register of Historic Places Inventory – Nomination Form, Morgan –Bedinger- Dandridge House," March 29, 1983. Retrieved from http://www.wvculture.org/shpo/nr/pdf/jefferson/83003239.pdf
94 Morgan, Mary Ann, personal communication, August 1, 2017.

CHAPTER 5 FARM LANDLORDS

OUR STORY WILL now turn to some of the early farmhouse owners who we know were absentee landlords. While trying to learn more about the first of these owners, Walter B. Selby, I inadvertently blundered upon the original owner of the house. Once that discovery is behind us, I will construct a comprehensive historical record of accessible material about all the farm's non-resident owners through 1946, when the farmhouse finally passed out of the Selby and Hamtramck families and became owner-occupied.

Selby and Hamtramck Families

The Walter Bowie Selby and John Francis Hamtramck families had ties to our farmhouse for most of the nineteenth and the first half of the twentieth centuries. Walter Selby was the earliest documented owner of the house I could find—his name appearing on S. Howell Brown's 1852 Jefferson County tax map linking him with it. In 1825, John Hamtramck married into the Selby family, and eventually, the farmhouse passed down through his offspring until 1946.

Late in my research, I discovered a collection of personal papers named the "John Francis Hamtramck Papers, 1757–1862." Duke University's David M. Rubenstein Rare Book and Manuscript Library holds this collection, and it is available to the public. It contains many letters and other documents, which reveal personal details of the lives of members of both the Selby and Hamtramck families. I will present most of the material I found interesting from the collection in the next chapter. Nonetheless, I offer a limited amount of it in this chapter where it fits this part of the story better.

The Rubenstein Library also holds other collections of personal and business papers from early Shepherdstown families. These include the Alexander Boteler Papers, 1707–1924; the Bedinger and Dandridge Family Papers, 1752–2000; the Abraham Shepherd Papers, 1782–1880; the James Rumsey Papers, 1785–1816; the Joseph Entler Papers, 1823–1878; and the Billmyer Family Papers, 1832–1906. I have not looked at any of these collections, but they may contain information that could help resolve some of the questions my research has left unanswered. Other researchers interested in learning more about early Shepherdstown life should know about these collections.

I will now continue to present here all the information I could gather on the lives of the owners of the farmhouse beginning with Walter Selby and proceeding to Florence Williamson Sampson. Florence Sampson sold the property in 1946 to a family that unquestionably occupied the house for the first time in well over a century. As the story unfolds, we will discover who the original owner of the farmhouse was and a reliable estimate of its construction date. I will enhance this information with more personal detail in the next chapter. The date ranges following the owners' names in the subheadings below are the years of their ownership, not of their life spans.

Walter B. Selby 1811–1855

We know that Walter B. Selby owned our log farmhouse in 1852 based on S. Howell Brown's tax map. However, this map offers no clue about when or from whom he acquired it. This is the earliest map showing a structure on the exact site of the present-day farmhouse. Two older and sketchier maps of the area dated 1809 and 1820 show a few farmhouses of the most prominent owners or those willing to pay to include themselves. However, our farmhouse does not appear on either of these maps leaving us to wonder who owned it before Walter Selby. We will solve this mystery in a few moments but first, let us learn more about Walter B. Selby.

Walter Selby arrived in Shepherdstown as a young man in the 1790's from Maryland, probably from Prince Georges County—his middle name was Bowie, a city in that county. He was not married at the time. He soon built up a prosperous dry goods business in town. His store's account book for 1795–1796 is held in the archives of the Historic Shepherdstown Museum. This book is a sizable leather-bound volume of several hundred pages. Two of its pages appear in Figure 5.1. The book includes accounts for Alen B. Selby and Thomas Selby, whose surname suggests that they were family members who either preceded, accompanied or followed Walter Selby to Shepherdstown. Alen, Thomas, and Walter Selby may have been brothers striking out for new opportunities on the frontier. Walter appears to have been the only one who stayed in Shepherdstown since Alen and Thomas did not appear in any other documents I examined.

From Walter Selby's account book, we know that he sold items like bar iron, cloth, muslin, tea, coffee, salt, stone pots, candles, wheat, rye, cheese, and brandy. Bar iron appears in many orders, probably for fashioning into parts for repair of equipment or making into household items. Widow Morgan's account displayed in the illustration undoubtedly was that of Colonel William Morgan's widow, George Morgan's mother, and Walter Selby's future mother-in-law.

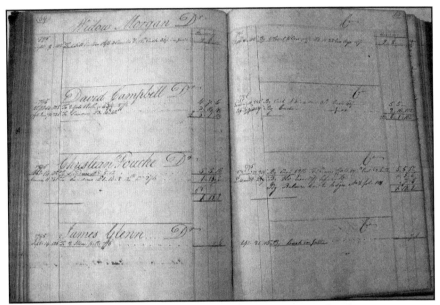

FIGURE 5.1 Selby dry goods store 1795–1796 account book pages.
Courtesy of the Historic Shepherdstown Commission. Credit: Joseph Goss.

Reverend Dr. Moses Hoge, the first Presbyterian minister of Shepherdstown, officiated the marriage of Walter Selby to Eleanor Morgan (1782–1820) on Christmas Eve 1797.[95] Could Walter Selby have somehow acquired the log farmhouse through his marriage to the daughter of the man who obtained the original land grant where it stands? Not exactly, as we will soon see. Reverend Hoge, pictured in Figure 5.2, served in Shepherdstown from 1787 to 1807, afterward becoming president of Hampden-Sydney College in Virginia. John Randolph,

---

95 West Virginia Vital Research Records, "Marriage Record Detail." Retrieved from http://www.wvculture.org/vrr/va_mcdetail.aspx?Id=12492065

a Virginia congressman, claimed that Reverend Hoge "was the most eloquent man I ever heard in the pulpit or out of it."[96]

As mentioned earlier, I obtained copies of every deed —twenty-nine in all—in Berkeley and Jefferson Counties that name a Selby as the grantee or the deceased in a division-of-property deed. I wanted to see if I could find among them the deeds revealing Walter Selby's purchase of the farmhouse property and who received it on his death. After painstakingly transcribing a few of these documents, some scarcely legible, I postponed work on the rest until later in hopes of finding a more accessible path to the information I sought.

FIGURE 5.2 Reverend Dr. Moses Hoge. *Courtesy of Shepherdstown Presbyterian Church.*

After exhausting all my other potential sources— newspapers, local historical society journals, historical accounts written by local authors, and internet searches—I decided to give the Berkeley County Historical Society's files one more try. This final desperate effort produced an unexpected windfall. From an obscure record in the vault room, I found an unsigned, undated, handwritten and nearly illegible page of research notes about the neighboring Aspen Pool farm to the east of our farmhouse. Near the end of the page, the author casually refers to the house west of Aspen Pool on the 1852 tax map as George Morgan's house.[97]

---

96 Wikipedia contributors, "Moses Hoge." Retrieved from https://en.wikipedia.org/wiki/Moses_Hoge

97 Wood, Don C., written communication, undated. BCHS Survey File S-85.

I knew this was our house. I had found the "holy grail" of my quest. I asked volunteers at the Berkeley County Historical Society if they could name the author of the handwritten notes. Several of them verified that it was the late distinguished historian and genealogist, Don C. Wood, based on their long-time personal acquaintance with him and his handwriting. These notes were a vital discovery. On further inspection, I found a copy of a deed in the same file transferring a one-third interest in a 200-acre tract formerly owned by George Morgan, deceased, from his son, Rawleigh Morgan Jr., to Walter B. Selby in 1811. He paid the unusual amount of $2,333.33, probably meaning the full price of the property would have been $7,000.

Although this deed did not mention the house, it proved a connection between the 200 acres George Morgan's father granted him in 1788 and our log farmhouse. The 1788 will describes the 200-acre tract given to George as the one upon which he then lived. The three documents consisting of Colonel William Morgan's 1788 will, the 1811 deed, and Don Wood's notes present unassailable proof that George Morgan was the first owner of our farmhouse. I had achieved one of my primary objectives. It did not reveal itself directly but took a process of document triangulation and some luck to discover.

Colonel Morgan's will positively dates the house at least as far back as 1788, which moves us closer to its received date of 1780. Since we know that George Morgan was already living in the house in 1788, it is reasonable to believe that he had been living there before that year. To move this line of reasoning forward, I consulted the marriage records in Berkeley County, which go back to 1781. George Morgan's marriage to Drusilla Swearingen does not appear in them. However, Drusilla's two unions following George's death in 1796 are there. I conclude from these facts that George and Drusilla married before 1781. If they built their house around the time of their marriage, the dwelling has a secure claim to construction in 1780 if not even earlier.

The house had only been in the hands of five unrelated families before our ownership—comparatively few for its age. This fact advances the likelihood of the 1780 date having come down by word of mouth. Jefferson County lists the house as built in 1780, although the assessor's office relies on the owners of an old home to supply its age. Based on all these indications, I suggest that 1780 is a reasonable date for the house and is as near as it is possible to fix the year of its construction. I conclude that the George Morgan House easily merits a date of circa 1780 if we define it to mean a commonly used range of five years before or after the postulated year.

I can imagine an earlier date for the house—perhaps 1759. As I mentioned in Chapter 2, Colonel Morgan could have built it as his settlement house within three years of the 1756 land grant to comply with the 1713 Acts of Virginia. Since he erected his stone house—Springdale Farm—around 1760, this theory seems implausible but not impossible.

There was still a slight nagging doubt in my mind whether George Morgan lived in his own house. The "Berkeley County Land Books of 1782–1803," mentioned in the previous chapter, list George Morgan owning one lot and receiving rent in 1787. Since these land books give no other details, we cannot be sure if this lot was the site of our farmhouse or some other property that George Morgan owned and rented out.

Another possibility is that the land books listing for George Morgan was for our farmhouse property, that George Morgan lived in the farmhouse as of 1787, and that he rented out part of the land. This scenario seems the most likely to me since there is no evidence that he owned any other property. However, it does not resolve why he would have been taxed for property that his father apparently still owned until his 1788 death.

My next step was to go back, unenthusiastically as foretold in Chapter 1, to transcribe and write extracts of all the Selby deeds I had collected early in my research. I hoped to find the one-third interest deed of 1811 and others among them to piece together the missing parts of Walter Selby's purchase of George Morgan's farm. I have entered all these deed extracts in Appendix A and numbered them for easy referencing in the text. For example, the 1811 deed extract is No. 8 in Appendix A.

I found two more deeds that completed Walter Selby's purchase of George Morgan's 200-acre property—one dated 1815 (No. 14) and the other dated 1817 (No. 15)—for considerations of $5,000 each. Heirs of George Morgan granted both deeds—each for a one-third interest in the property.

Thus, it took Walter Selby six years to acquire full ownership of the log house and farm—George Morgan's home place. Walter Selby might have used his farm and several other large parcels he gained over the years as part of the supply chain for the Selby dry goods store.

Another deed confirms that Walter Selby did not live at the log farmhouse. The year before he began purchasing our farm he bought the Wynkoop Tavern from Rawleigh Morgan—son of Colonel William Morgan—and his wife Elizabeth (Deed No. 6). This edifice is the elegant brick mansion that appears in Figure 5.3 and which stands on German Street. It befitted a prosperous businessman, such as Selby was at that time, far more than George Morgan's rustic log farmhouse.

In addition to finding the earliest recorded deeds to our farm property, I managed to map with reasonable certainty the boundaries of George Morgan's 200-acre farm using a web-based software program. I describe this

FIGURE 5.3 Wynkoop Tavern, 2017. *Credit: Joseph Goss.*

mapping process in detail in the extract for Deed No. 8 where I also present a plot of the farm's boundaries superimposed on a current map.

The Wynkoop Tavern has a storied history going back to 1769. Cornelius Wynkoop built the present imposing structure in 1792, either replacing or incorporating the original tavern.[98] The Wynkoop Tavern may have served as one of Shepherdstown's theaters for a time.

A 1791 ad in the *Potomak Guardian and Berkeley Advertiser* publicized the famous comedy of manners entitled "The Contrast," followed by "The Waterman; or, Who Rules the Roost." The ad says that patrons can buy tickets at Mr. Wynkoop's Tavern. Citizens commonly found all types of

98 Musser, 165.

entertainment in taverns at that time, so it is not surprising that such a show would take place at the Wynkoop Tavern. The ad appears in Figure 5.4. Notice the final line in Latin meaning "May the republic flourish."[99]

I looked up the current owners of the Wynkoop Tavern to see if they might have any information on Walter Selby or his family and descendants. The present owners have lived in the house for eighteen years. They invited us to tour their home on June 15, 2017, and to ask questions about its history relating to the Selby family. The homeowner was aware of the Selby ownership of the house but had never heard of our farmhouse or that Walter Selby had owned it too. He said that he had served as president of the Historic Shepherdstown Museum in the past and had turned over several documents he had found in the house to the Museum.

FIGURE 5.4 Advertisement for "The Contrast," 1791. *Image courtesy of Berkeley County Historical Society microfilm archives.*

One of these documents might have been Walter Selby's 1795–1796 account book. On the inside of the front cover of the book, an undated handwritten note reads "Walter Bowie Selby's Ledger #1—Given to J. H. S. Billmeyer by Gran." James Henry Shepherd Billmeyer (1903–1976) was a great-grandson of

---

99 McGrath's Company of Comedians, "The Contrast," advertisement, *Potomak Guardian and Berkeley Advertiser*, July 11, 1791, 3.

Colonel Hamtramck and great-great-grandson of Walter B. Selby. The "Gran" in the inscription must be Florence Hamtramck Shepherd (1836–1918)—a one-time owner of our house—according to an extensive handwritten, unsigned, and undated Hamtramck family tree. This family tree traces the Hamtramcks from 1756 through 1989 and resides in the archives of the Historic Shepherdstown Museum. It is undoubtedly the work of an unknown modern descendant. More about Florence Shepherd follows toward the end of this chapter. It is not recorded how the account book found its way from J. H. S. Billmeyer to the Historic Shepherdstown Museum. However, it might have been left behind in the Wynkoop Tavern and been among the things the present homeowner donated.

The Wynkoop Tavern is grand in scale with soaring ceilings and a spacious center hall with two large rooms on either side. All four chambers have fireplaces with ornate wooden mantles. The rooms to the right of the center hall are the living and dining rooms. To its left are two spaces of unequal size, which now connect with each other. The broad opening between them has an ornate fluted column at each end. The current homeowner believes Walter Selby joined these rooms for banquets and balls. A kitchen added years ago attaches to the rear of the main house. To the back of this kitchen is the original stone-built kitchen, modernized and still in use.

To the rear of the old stone-built kitchen is a room with a beehive oven accessible only from the outside. To the back of the oven room is a smoke room for curing meats. It features vertical vent slits built into the brick walls. To the rear of the smoke room are two privies, one for the women and girls and the other for the men and boys. These privies are three-seaters with no partitions. We did not inspect their interiors, but there is a picture of one in *Uncommon Vernacular*.[100] All the rooms behind and including the old stone-built kitchen might have been part of the original 1769 tavern.

I tried to trace the Wynkoop Tavern's deeds back in time from the present but came to a dead end in 1986. The tavern did not leave the hands of Selby and Hamtramck family descendants until that year. The 1986

---

100 Allen, 151.

deed cites the property as being the same one sold to Walter B. Selby by Rawleigh and Elizabeth Morgan in 1810 (Deed No. 6). No recorded deeds to the tavern exist between 1810 and 1986.[101]

Allegedly, famous guests visited the Wynkoop Tavern many times. George Washington, not yet president, traveled to Shepherdstown to witness the trial of James Rumsey's steam-powered boat on the Potomac River in 1784. According to legend, the tavern hosted and entertained Washington as well as Thomas Jefferson.[102] In 1910, a writer for the *Shepherdstown Register* related stories some townspeople told him, which their ancestors had handed down to them. One of these stories recounted how "Washington and Lafayette sat together at the open fire-place in high conference," at the Wynkoop Tavern.[103] The present homeowner, however, said he doubted these stories without citing a reason. I neither searched for nor found primary sources that could confirm them.

I want to deviate slightly from the main narrative here. The story of Washington and Lafayette signals the first of numerous articles that I will cite in this and coming chapters, which I found through the Library of Congress's extraordinary "Chronicling America" project. The articles appeared in the *Spirit of Jefferson* and the *Shepherdstown Register*, two local newspapers the Library of Congress has digitized and made searchable online as part of the project.

To reduce redundancy, whenever I reference articles from these two newspapers in the footnotes, I have abbreviated their source as "LOC Chronicling America." The general web address for this material is *https://chroniclingamerica.loc.gov/*. The full citation for these articles should read "Library of Congress, Chronicling America: Historic American Newspapers site," followed by the web address for each article.[104] However, for footnote brevity, I will not include all this material.

---

101 Jefferson County Clerk, *Deed Book 570*, Page 292, November 5, 1986.

102 McC., W., staff correspondent, "Noted House is Reminder of Bygone Day," *Baltimore Sun*, November 25, 1926, 98

103 *Shepherdstown Register*, Shepherdstown, W.Va., September 22, 1910,1. LOC Chronicling America.

104 Library of Congress, Chronicling America, About the Site and API. Retrieved from https://chroniclingamerica.loc.gov/about/api/

It is outright providential that the two cited periodicals—the only local ones—should be among the 2,684 historical newspapers that the Library of Congress has rendered searchable. It is even more astonishing that they come from the library's extensive database of over one hundred and fifty thousand historical newspapers published between 1690 and the present. The Chronicling America project, however, does not include the *Martinsburg Gazette*. Fortunately, the Berkeley County Historical Society has a manually-generated index of this newspaper—the work of a dedicated volunteer in the 1970's to whom I am indebted.

Elise Shepherd Billmyer, daughter of Florence Shepherd, inherited the Wynkoop Tavern on her mother's death in 1918. She claimed that W. W. Corcoran (1798–1888), founder of the now-closed Corcoran Gallery in Washington, D.C., and financier and philanthropist, George Peabody (1795–1869), were frequent visitors at the house and unsuccessful aspirants for the hand of Sally Selby, one of Walter's daughters.[105] This report is somewhat confusing as the Selbys' only daughters were Eliza Claggett (1805–1839), Eleanor (1810–unk.), and Sarah Eleanor (1812–1889). Nevertheless, there is a corroborating piece in a 1976 publication telling that Mrs. Sally Selby Hamtramck inherited the house from her father, Walter B. Selby.[106] Also, an 1837 deed—not included in Appendix A—identifies Sarah Eleanor Selby as Sally.[107] I conclude that Sarah Eleanor Selby and Sally—or Sallie—Selby were the same woman.

I could not figure out where Walter Selby lived between the 1790's and 1810 when he bought the Wynkoop Tavern. The 1798 Federal House and Slave Tax lists him owning one house in Shepherdstown valued at $420. This value was far above average compared with other Berkeley County houses, although it did not stand out as one of the most valuable and doubtless more magnificent dwellings. He also held one slave in 1798.

Another mystery from the 1798 House and Slave Tax is that it lists a Mary Cary as the occupant of Selby's house instead of *self*. The 1798 tax list records the occupant as *self*, meaning the owner, for most houses. Also, Walter Selby shows up in the same 1798 tax list as the occupant of one of

---

105 McC., W.

106 The Bicentennial Commission, "See Shepherd's Town," 1976, 28. Scarborough Library, Jefferson County Special Collection, Shepherd University.

107 Pendleton, 15.

Abraham Shepherd's houses in town. Abraham owned two houses in the country and two in town. Shepherd occupied the more valuable of his two homes in town.[108]

This house must have been Abraham's large brick house, which stands on East High Street. The scant information about Deed No. 1 in Appendix A comes from a surviving index to Berkeley County's *Deed Book No. 14* (1797–1798). It lists the lease of a lot, possibly including a house, in Shepherdstown, which a Shepherd—probably Abraham—granted to Walter Selby. *Deed Book No. 14* happens to be Berkeley County's only lost deed book. Some believe that people burned or stole it during the Civil War. This deed could have been for Walter Selby's first residence in town or his first store. Could he have owned another house in Shepherdstown, as suggested in the 1798 tax list, with an unrecorded deed? I will leave these questions to others, as they take us too far afield from the focus of this project.

The Berkeley County property tax list for 1800 lists Walter Selby's household with one white, no slaves, one horse, and one head of cattle for which the tax was fifty-six pence. In 1801, his homestead consisted of two whites, one slave, one horse, and one head of cattle for which the charge was $2.11. This does not help us learn any more about where he lived at that time. The accuracy of these early tax lists is shaky in my view as the first one seems to omit Walter Selby's wife and first son and the second one appears to exclude the first and second son.

Walter and Eleanor Morgan Selby had at least five sons besides their three daughters—William Morgan Selby (1799–1833[109]), Walter Bowie Selby Jr. (1801–1839), Thomas Swearingen Selby (1803–unk.), John Claggett Selby (1808–unk.), and Henry Swearingen Selby (1814–1898). An assumed son named James Monroe Selby (1817–unk.) was born at the beginning of his namesake's presidency.[110] I say *assumed* because only one source mentions this son and he is absent from all other sources in which the Selby children are named.

---

108 Wood, Don C., transcriber, "1798 House and Slave Tax of Berkeley County Virginia," undated, 19.

109 Historical Records Survey Box 5, undated. BCHS microfilm archives.

110 Pendleton, 11.

In 1884, Mr. H. Hunt wrote to the *Shepherdstown Register* from Montpelier, Indiana, that he had lived in Shepherdstown from 1830 to 1835 and that those were some of the happiest years of his life. Among many other people of the town, he reminisced about some young men his same age at that time. Mr. Hunt knew three of Walter B. Selby's sons—Henry, Thomas, and Walter Jr. He described Walter Jr. as quite intelligent and something of a politician who, a Democrat, had heated discussions with Archie Cameron, a Whig, over tariffs. Thomas, on the other hand, was entirely different. When they had chicken fights at Mrs. Weltzheimer's tavern, he enthusiastically led the Shepherdstown side. Hunt wrote nothing about Henry other than he thought all three boys would have passed away.[111] Henry had not and must have seen Hunt's letter.

A new figure who would have far-reaching impact entered the Selby family in 1825. Colonel John Francis Hamtramck (1798–1858) married Eliza Claggett Selby on December 1, 1825.[112] She was his second wife. Sarah Eleanor (aka Sally) Selby became John F. Hamtramck's third wife on October 25, 1842, in Frederick, Maryland, following her sister Eliza's death in 1839—the same year as Walter Bowie Selby Jr.'s death.[113]

Eliza Claggett gave birth to her last child, Sarah Frances (Eliza) Hamtramck, in February 1839. Sadly, Eliza Claggett died only two months later. Her untimely demise could mean she died of causes related to childbirth. However, her death notice only mentions:

> [T]he generous impulses of her nature gave to her society an interesting and instructive attraction. . . . [She was] [e]arly impressed with the truths and mysteries of the Holy Catholic Religion. . . . Her death was most exemplary . . . the scene replete with consolation. . . . Almost her last breath bore aloft a prayer and . . . she sang in a faint, sweet, tremulous voice, the praises to her Saviour.[114]

---

111 *Shepherdstown Register*, Shepherdstown, W.Va., January 26, 1884, 3. LOC Chronicling America.

112 File folder, "Descendants of Walter Bowie Selby," Historic Shepherdstown & Museum archives, Selby Family Folder, 1.

113 *Martinsburg Gazette*, Martinsburg, Va., November 4, 1842, 3. BCHS microfilm archives.

114 Death notice, *Martinsburg Gazette*, Martinsburg, Va., April 17, 1839, 2. BCHS microfilm archives.

A writer portrays Sarah Frances in her old age as a delicate little lady who swathed herself in shawls for fear of taking cold. She implored her friends to "beware of wet feet because Miss Sally Welshans was found dead in her bed."[115] The Welshans family had a women's clothing store on the south side of East German Street where a building still stands with the Welshans name inscribed across a false front above the second floor. Sarah Frances eventually came to own our farmhouse with her older sister, Florence.

Two Possible Sites of the Selby Store

FIGURE 5.5 East German Street, late nineteenth century. *Image courtesy of the Historic Shepherdstown Commission.*

The Selby dry goods store stood on Lot No. 34 in town. A 1986 article claims to show the stone house that may have been the store—the fourth building from the street corner on the right in the photograph presented in Figure 5.5.[116] The article says that Walter Selby might have rented his store before he bought it in 1804.[117] Deed No. 4 in Appendix A may confirm this

---

115 Pendleton, 11.

116 German Street Looking West from Princess Street, photograph, Historic Shepherdstown & Museum archives, undated.

117 "The Shepherdstown of Philip Adam Entler," *Spirit Of Jefferson Farmer's Advocate*, October 9, 1986, 9.

purchase. The photograph is from the late nineteenth century judging by the men's attire and lack of automobiles, street paving, telephone lines, or electric streetlights. Shepherdstown did not receive electric service until 1902.[118] The fire of 1912 destroyed at least two buildings in the photograph including the third and fourth buildings from the intersection.

Long after reading the 1986 article, I found another source written in 2012 by James C. Price, historian laureate of Shepherdstown. Dr. Price's book includes an old photograph of the same scene as that in Figure 5.5, but it was taken some years later. His photo caption identifies the fifth

FIGURE 5.6 East German Street, 2017. *Credit: Joseph Goss.*

building from the intersection in Figure 5.5—a brick house—as the Selby-Lambright-Reinhart Building [119] I hoped to contact Dr. Price to ask if he had any further information about the Selby-Lambright-Reinhart Building being the site of Walter Selby's store, but he had died over a year before I picked up his book.

I compared the original town lot numbers with current property lines along this block of East German Street. The original lot lines do not map onto the current ones; however, the combined frontage dimensions of the

118 Surkamp, James T., "Events and Dates from Prehistoric to Present Times, Jefferson County, West Virginia," poster, author's collection, 2001.

119 Price, James C., ...*and so I did. Stories of Shepherdstown*, Volume I, self published, 2012, 69.

old and current lots do add up. In fact, the side lot lines of old Lot No. 34 still exist even though the old lot comprises three lots facing East German Street today. When I superimposed current property lines onto satellite mapping, it is clear those three lots included both the fourth and fifth buildings from the intersection in the photograph. Given Dr. Price's caption, the 1986 article, and mapping the old lot lines onto a current map, either of those two buildings—indicated in Figure 5.5—could have been the site of Walter Selby's store.

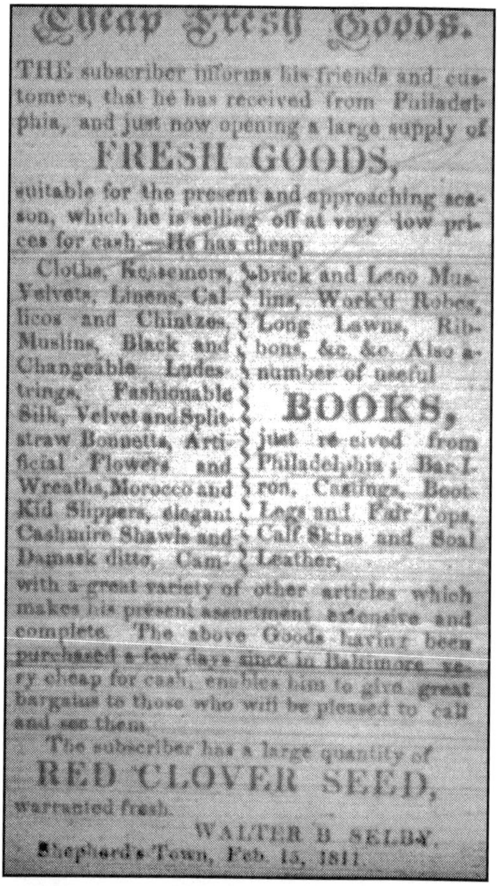

FIGURE 5.7 Selby dry goods advertisement, 1811. *Image courtesy of Berkeley County Historical Society microfilm archives.*

The same view of German Street in 2017 appears in Figure 5.6. A wood-frame building has replaced the stone house (fourth from the corner), and a two-story brick building has replaced the Selby-Lambright-Reinhart Building in the earlier photograph. Built the year after the 1912 fire, the three-story Masonic Temple between the two buildings obscures all but the weather vane atop the tower of McMurran Hall.

I will now present some more details of Walter Selby's life gathered from public records and a variety of publications. In 1811, he placed the ad exhibited in Figure 5.7 in the *Martinsburg Gazette* for "Cheap Fresh Goods."[120] These goods included velvets, linens, muslins, silk,

---

120 Selby, Walter B., "Cheap Fresh Goods," advertisement, *Martinsburg Gazette*, Martinsburg, Va., February 15, 1811, 3. BCHS microfilm archives.

bonnets, ribbons, cashmere shawls, bar iron, castings, clover seed, and some "Useful Books," which he had bought a few days before in Baltimore. Some of the same types of items also appeared on the pages of his 1795–1796 account book presented previously in this chapter.

Walter Selby reported a theft from the stillhouse at his farm—most likely our farmhouse property—in 1814. He offered a thirty-dollar reward for the return of a red Morocco pocketbook containing cash plus many promissory notes from customers.[121] The stillhouse suggests a reason he bought the farm since it was not for a place to live. As I have already proposed, he could have used it to supply some of the goods he sold at his store in town, such as various grains and, of course, whiskey.

Farm owner Walter Selby lived in town leading me to wonder who lived and worked at his farm during its long period of absentee ownership. My research was finally able to answer this in part. I will postpone those stories until an upcoming chapter. For now, I can say that Walter Selby let the farm out to tenants who lived in the log house, worked the fields, and might have hired other hands or used enslaved laborers.

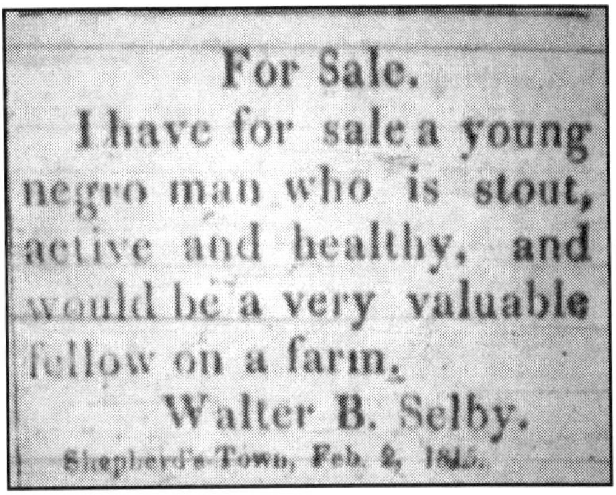

For Sale.

I have for sale a young negro man who is stout, active and healthy, and would be a very valuable fellow on a farm.

Walter B. Selby.

Shepherd's Town, Feb. 2, 1815.

FIGURE 5.8 Selby slave advertisement, 1815. *Image courtesy of Berkeley County Historical Society microfilm archives.*

We know through tax and census records that Walter Selby held slaves. We also have the 1815 newspaper ad displayed in Figure 5.8, which shows he had slaves to work his farm.[122] The Berkeley County property tax list of 1800 lists him owning one slave over sixteen, as already noted. The U.S. Census of 1810 records him owning five slaves. The 1810 census also tells us that there were two adults under forty-five—Walter and Eleanor—seven children under ten and two young

---

121 Daugherty, Samuel, "Thirty Dollars Reward," advertisement, *Martinsburg Gazette*, Martinsburg, Va., March 17, 1814. BCHS microfilm archives.
122 Selby, Walter B., "For Sale," advertisement, *Martinsburg Gazette*, Martinsburg, Va., February 2, 1815. BCHS microfilm archives.

men in his household.[123] The Selbys had only six children by 1810, so the seventh child and two men listed are unknown. Altogether, this household lodged sixteen people including the slaves. Walter Selby bought the Wynkoop Tavern in September 1810, implying he still lived at his leased property (Deed No. 1) as of the official date of the 1810 census—August 6. Since he had not bought his farm yet, Walter Selby must have employed his five slaves at his residence, in his dry goods business, leased them out, or a combination of these.

The 1820 U.S. Census tells that there were seven free whites and four slaves in the Selby household at the Wynkoop Tavern. This census tells us that Walter was a merchant, three members of his homestead worked in commerce, and none worked in agriculture or manufacturing.[124] Besides their father, Walter's two oldest sons could have worked in his store.

Since no one in the household worked in agriculture, the listed slaves might have worked in the house or the store. Walter Selby could also have owned slaves who lived and worked at our farm, but the census would likely have counted them with the farm household. But when I looked up the farm's tenant in the 1820 census I found he had no slaves.[125] The Selby household had shrunk by five since the 1810 census. I will disclose more information about Walter Selby and his family's connections with slavery in Chapter 6. In Chapter 8, we will consider the subject of slavery at the Selby farm in particular.

Walter Selby occupied a prominent place in the public life of Shepherdstown. At the eighth Shepherdstown election, held the first Monday of April 1801, the town named him treasurer and re-elected him to that post at the ninth town election in 1802. On March 12, 1803, the town meeting ordered him to procure a fire engine and to pay any further sums that might be necessary. The town meeting held on September 4, 1809, requested that people be hired to level German Street "agreeably to the highest part of the street between Phillip Shutt's and Walter Selby's

---

123 Archive.org, "Population Schedules of the Third Census of the United State, 1810, Virginia," microform, 379. Retrieved from https://archive.org/stream /populationschedu0069unix#page/n378/mode/1up

124 Watts, Donald E., compiler and transcriber, "Fourth Census of the United States of America, 1820," October 2012, 37. BCHS microfilm archives.

125 1820 U.S. Census, record of John Sigler household. Retrieved from https://www .familysearch.org/ark:/61903/3:1:33S7-9YYY-SJF?i=3&cc=1803955

and to the highest ground between Thomas Toole's and James Brown's in the center of the street." The town then authorized Walter Selby to have the street leveling done.[126]

The fifteenth town meeting elected Walter Selby trustee and treasurer on the first Monday of April 1808. At the seventeenth town election in 1810, citizens elected him a trustee. A town meeting on April 5, 1813, directed Walter Selby, Swearingen—presumably Thomas Van Swearingen—and others to pay for "divers orders."[127]

On May 14, 1817, the following notice appeared in the *Charles Town Farmers' Repository*:

> The Co-partnership that existed under the firm of Selby and Swearingen, was dissolved in July last by its own limitation – All those who stand indebted to said firm are requested to make payment to Walter B. Selby, who settles for the concern all transactions relative to same.

Walter B. Selby and Thomas Van Swearingen signed it.[128] This notice did not signal the end of the Selby business. Walter was only forty-six at the time. Still, I found no published advertisements for his business later than the one of 1811 illustrated previously. The 1817 notice could suggest a falling out with or merely the departure of his partner.

In 1857, the *Shepherdstown Register* obtained an old article related to the Selby business partnership from an early Shepherdstown publication named the *American Eagle*. It reported that by 1818, Walter Selby was in a partnership business called Selby & Wysong. The article also told that the partnership was soliciting to buy 4,000 bushels of flax seed while announcing the arrival of new goods at the store.[129]

Continuing his civic duties, on May 1, 1820, Walter Selby sat on a grand jury that indicted Jane Towlerton for selling spirituous liquors without a license. On March 17, 1821, a special meeting of the Common Hall of Shepherdstown elected Walter Selby as alderman to serve out the

---

126 Musser, 35–46.

127 Musser, 43–68.

128 Selby, Walter B., business notice, *Charles Town Farmers' Repository*, Vol. X, Issue 475, May 14, 1817, 4. Retrieved from http://www.geneaologybank.com/gbnk/newspapers /doc/v2:1044E5F20...

129 *Shepherdstown Register*, Shepherdstown, Va., April 4, 1857, 2. LOC Chronicling America.

remaining term of John B. Henry. On April 3, 1821, it chose him as alderman in his own right. On April 3, 1822, citizens elected Walter Selby mayor of Shepherdstown for the following year.[130]

Let us now take another look at census records of the Selby household to see what changes were happening at home. The 1830 U.S. Census of the Selby household counts four sons and no daughters living with widower Walter Selby. Before 1850, U.S. censuses did not record the names of those living in the house except for the head-of-household. However, in 1830, the sons at home—based on their ages—were William, Walter, Henry, and either Thomas or John. I could not learn which of the latter two had departed home—or succumbed—or anything about son James.

In 1830, daughter Eliza Claggett was in St. Louis with her husband, who was then Indian agent for the Osage Nation. Eliza's sister, Sally, who paid her visits in St. Louis, might have been on such a stay at the time of the 1830 census. Eleanor must have left home or died since the census counted no daughters at home. The 1830 census also counts one older male slave and three young female slaves forming a household of nine.[131]

The year 1839 was not a good one for the Selby family. It lost two adult children that year—first Eliza Claggett Selby Hamtramck and then Walter Bowie Selby Jr. I found this poignant death notice for Walter Jr.:

> At Shepherdstown, at the residence of his father, on Saturday 9th inst., of pulmonary consumption [tuberculosis], Walter B. Selby, Jr. in the 39th year of his age. After many months of severe suffering, which he bore with fortitude and resignation, without ever a murmur or complaint dropping from his lips, thus has passed away, in the meridian of life, one highly gifted in intellect, and when in health, rich in the social qualities of the heart.[132]

This rings true with the description of Walter Jr. that H. Hunt sent to the *Shepherdstown Register* years later, which I mentioned previously in this chapter.

The 1840 U.S. Census of the Selby household counts two sons and one daughter living with Walter Selby. The sons would be Henry, and either

---

130 Musser, 43–68.

131 1830 U.S. Census, record of Walter B. Selby household. Retrieved from http://www.wvgeohistory.org/Search.aspx#v=1707-census-1830

132 *Alexandria Gazette*, Alexandria, Va., November 25, 1839, 3.

Thomas or John, based on their ages. Sally was the only daughter living with her father at the time of this census. The census counts only one older female slave yielding a household of five—a decline of four since 1830.[133]

A minor item, dated 1843, turned up in the John Francis Hamtramck Papers—a receipt showing that Walter Selby paid $2.50 for a year's subscription to the *Virginia Free Press*.[134] This periodical was a weekly newspaper published in Charles Town from 1832 till 1916. At least we know he was keeping up with the times, but I found nothing else about Walter Selby between 1840 and 1845 from any source.

Three more years pass before we hear again of Walter Selby's activities in Shepherdstown. At a council meeting on July 11, 1846, he complained that he and John B. Woltz were apprehensive of danger from Dr. Taylor's board kiln. The council resolved that Dr. Taylor remove his furnace forthwith. On July 14, 1846, Walter Selby again complained of a board kiln put up by Dr. Taylor on his lot. The council decided Dr. Taylor could continue drying his boards provided he get a competent person to attend to them and that he have the fires put out every night by ten o'clock. I cannot tell whether Dr. Taylor's board kiln was near Selby's store or the Wynkoop Tavern without further deed research on the lots next to those buildings.

On May 24, 1847, Walter Selby among others petitioned the town council not to assess and levy any taxes on the town's citizens for that year as it had until then been "quite burdensome on them."[135] We may infer that at age seventy-seven Walter Selby was no longer engaged in business and might not have had the means he once had.

The 1850 U.S. Census lists Walter Selby as being eighty years old and having no occupation. Only one offspring, Henry, still lived with his father at that time. The same census lists Henry as literate, owning no slaves,

133 1840 U.S. Census, record of Walter B. Selby household. Retrieved from www
.wvgeohistory.org/Search.aspx#v=767-census-1840

134 Selby, Walter B., receipt, *Virginia Free Press* subscription, January 1, 1843. John Francis Hamtramck Papers, David M. Rubenstein Rare Book & Manuscript Library, Duke University.

135 Musser, 77–78.

and having no occupation.[136] The separate 1850 U.S. Slave Census lists three slaves in the household, the oldest being a sixty-year-old female mulatto.[137] Slave names never appeared in census data, although we see some in letters, wills, deeds, and ads for the return of runaways.

The final trace of the living Walter B. Selby appeared in the *Shepherdstown Register* in 1855, less than a month before his death. It advertised:

> [C]heap Dry Goods and Fancy Articles [offered by] D. I. Goldenberg & Co., from Baltimore . . . now opening at Mr. Selby's Store Room. . . . Goldenberg & Co. want to SELL OUT, . . . call soon and get the cream of the Bargains, as their stay will be very short.[138]

This clearly indicates that Walter Selby was no longer in the dry goods business at age eighty-five, although he still retained his old store. The advertisement proves that he rented his store out to other merchants, perhaps on a short-term basis as the Goldenberg & Co. ad implies.

Although he was a prominent member of the community for many years, people seemed to have largely forgotten Walter Selby by the time of his death on August 1, 1855, at age eighty-five. I found no death notices for him in the *Martinsburg Gazette* or the *Spirit of Jefferson* newspapers. A sole death notice appeared in the *Shepherdstown Register*:

> In this place, on Wednesday last, the 1st inst., Mr. Walter B. Selby, for a long time one of the principal Merchants of this place, aged about 85 years.[139]

Most death notices of the time were a paragraph long consisting of impersonal but inspirational language extolling the virtues of the deceased. Walter Selby did not even receive this token dignity, although in 1839, as pointed out earlier, both his son, Walter Jr., and daughter, Eliza Claggett, did. It is a sad testimony to the fleeting importance of a once prominent man.

---

136 1850 U.S. Census, record of Walter B. Selby household. Retrieved from http://familysearch.org/pal:/MM9.3.1/TH-266-11594-139033-78?cc

137 1850 U.S. Slave Census, record of Walter B. Selby household. Retrieved from http://www.wvgeohistory.org/Search.aspx#v=1318-census-1850s

138 *Shepherdstown Register*, Shepherdstown, Va., July 7, 1855, 3. LOC Chronicling America.

139 Selby, Walter B., death notice, *Shepherdstown Register*, August 4, 1855, 3. LOC Chronicling America.

The *Jefferson County Register of Deaths* discloses that the cause of Walter Selby's death was old age, he was born in Maryland, the names of his parents were unknown, his occupation was retired merchant, he was a widower, and the person giving the information of death was John F. Hamtramck, his son-in-law.[140] After Walter Selby's death, John and Sally Hamtramck moved into the Wynkoop Tavern.[141]

In 1856, Colonel Hamtramck advertised to sell or rent the deceased Walter Selby's storehouse and lot.[142] The following year we learn that John McEndree moved his old stand into Walter Selby's heirs' storehouse.[143] By then the storehouse belonged to Henry Selby among other heirs. Hence, McEndree was a tenant of the Selby storehouse for a time in the late 1850's. However, Henry did not sell it until 1874 (Deed No. 29).

I found an 1859 advertisement in the *Shepherdstown Register* that sheds light on the final disposal of Walter Selby's and Colonel Hamtramck's dry goods business. It announces:

CLOTHING! AT SHEPHERDSTOWN, VA.

The undersigned is now opening a LARGE STOCK of Ready-made Clothing, for Men and Boys (comprising Coats, Pants, and Vests, Shirts, Drawers, Cravats, Gloves, Socks, Suspenders, Shirt Collars, Pocket Handkerchiefs, Comforts, Shawls, Mourning Goods &c.) at the Store Room of Henry S. Selby, a few doors west of Entler's Hotel, Shepherdstown, to which he respectfully calls the attention of the public, as he is determined to SELL LOW FOR CASH.

JOHN G. STEPHENS, Agent.[144]

After Colonel Hamtramck's death in 1858, Henry S. Selby must have received the remaining stock of his father's and his brother-in-law's dry goods company. The location of the storeroom a "few doors west of

---

140 Selby, Walter B., record of death, *Jefferson County Register of Deaths 1853–1872*, line 39, 9.

141 Kenamond, 60.

142 *Shepherdstown Register*, Shepherdstown, Va., March 1, 1856, 1. LOC Chronicling America.

143 *Shepherdstown Register*, Shepherdstown, Va., April 4, 1857, 2. LOC Chronicling America.

144 *Shepherdstown Register*, Shepherdstown, Va., October 22, 1859, 3. LOC Chronicling America.

Entler's Hotel," matches the location of Walter Selby's store, which I found through other documents.

I tried to find a grave site for Walter Selby at Elmwood Cemetery, where one should be able to locate all the early Presbyterian burials. The caretaker perused the registry for me but could find no entry for his grave. Nevertheless, the caretaker did find an 1898 entry for Walter's son, Henry Swearingen Selby.

It appears that written wills—at least recorded ones—were not prevalent during the early years of our farmhouse. The only testaments I found from the Morgan family were from Captain Richard Morgan (1763) and Colonel William Morgan (1788). I saw no will or court-ordered division of property for George Morgan. Walter Selby did not record a will either, as I have mentioned previously, but the Jefferson County Court assigned overseers to divide his property. Deeds No. 27 and No. 28 describe a division of his property from which we learn that only two of his children received anything. Daughter Eliza Claggett preceded him in death, son Henry supplanted her and received our farm, while daughter Sally gained other lands via the court-supervised division. Sadly, all of Walter Selby's other children appear to have predeceased him.

No photographs of Walter Selby surfaced during my research, but I believe at least one may have existed. A photographer briefly set up shop above Walter's store as an 1850 advertisement proclaims:

> Mr. Macomber one of the oldest and most accomplished Daguerrean operators in the country has taken rooms over [Walter] Selby's Store, for a short time. His pictures in point of distinctness and beauty, exceed any ever yet exhibited in this place. Persons in want of a good likeness cannot do better than to give him a call.[145]

I found photographs of Walter Selby's daughter, Sally, and two granddaughters—both owners of our house. The 1867 photo in Figure 5.9 shows members of the Hamtramck and Selby families on the front porch of the Wynkoop Tavern. From the left, they are Miss Rebecca Young of Baltimore, Mrs. Eliza Hamtramck Williamson, Colonel Johnson of Baltimore (in top hat), Luke Tiernan Williamson of Baltimore, Mrs.

---

145 *Shepherdstown Register*, Shepherdstown, Va., November 12, 1850, 2. LOC Chronicling America.

Johnson, Florence Hamtramck Shepherd, James Hervey Shepherd, Mrs. John Francis Hamtramck (née Sarah Eleanor Selby, aka Sally), and Mami Sally, the cook. The photo looks blurry due to its original halftone source.

Rebecca must have been a family friend. She appears in letters from Colonel Hamtramck's second wife, Eliza Claggett Selby, and their daughter, Ellen Eliza. I will tell more about their letters in the next chapter. The occasion for the photograph was a house party soon after the marriage of James and Florence Shepherd.[146] Notice African American Mami Sally who only a few years earlier could have been the family's slave.

FIGURE 5.9 Selby–Hamtramck family post-wedding party at the Wynkoop Tavern, 1867. *Image courtesy of the West Virginia GeoExplorer Project.*

Sally Selby Hamtramck presented a stately figure all in black and seated to the right of the door in the photo. She is Colonel Hamtramck's widow, daughter of Walter B. Selby, and to my knowledge, the oldest Selby family member captured in a photograph. At the time of the photo, she was fifty-five years old and living in the house with her brother, Henry.

146 Family on front porch of Shepherd house, 204 East German Street, Shepherdstown, W.Va., 1867, photograph. Retrieved from http://www.wvgeohistory.org/Search.aspx#v=42907

She lost her husband in 1858—only three years after moving into the house. She and Colonel Hamtramck lost both of their children—Sallie McKenzie at age nineteen and Jesse Burgess Thomas in infancy according to the Hamtramck family tree held by the Historic Shepherdstown Museum. She died at home in 1889 after being in feeble health for a long time.[147]

Eliza Williamson evidently lived in Baltimore with her husband, but the newlyweds Florence and James Shepherd lived in Shepherdstown. It is possible that Eliza's husband, Luke Tiernan Williamson, was related to Colonel Hamtramck's first wife and her parents who were Williamsons from Baltimore. The 1867 date of the photograph compares correctly with the year of Florence Hamtramck's and James Shepherd's marriage recorded in the previously mentioned Hamtramck family tree. However, the names of the photo's subjects must have been written later, because Eliza Hamtramck was not yet Mrs. Williamson in 1867. A marriage notice in the *Spirit of Jefferson* reported the marriage of Mr. Luke T. Williamson, of Baltimore, and Miss Eliza Hamtramck at the residence of the bride's mother, incorrectly identified as Sally Selby Hamtramck, by Father O'Keefe on January 20, 1869. The 1867 photo caption misidentifying Eliza Hamtramck as Mrs. Eliza Hamtramck Williamson is likely due to its being written after their wedding in 1869.[148] The marriage announcement mistakes Sally Selby for her deceased sister, Eliza Claggett Selby Hamtramck—Eliza Hamtramck's Catholic mother.

Henry S. Selby 1855–1898

Following Walter Selby's death, his son, Henry, received the lot with the log farmhouse and the corn crib marked on a plan, which supplemented Deed No. 28. Henry's sister, Sally, got other property via the same deed. The corn crib that Henry received still stands, although it is now on a separate property adjacent to our farmhouse and is in disrepair. There is no mention in Deed No. 28 of the historic bank barn, also in disrepair, next to the corn crib, which was part of the Selby farm and now stands on the adjacent property. The 1883 S. Howell Brown tax map confirms Henry Selby's ownership of our farmhouse—it shows the house on the

---

147 *Shepherdstown Register*, Shepherdstown, W.Va., May 31, 1889, 2. LOC Chronicling America.

148 *Spirit of Jefferson*, Charles Town, W. Va., January 26, 1869, 2. LOC Chronicling America.

land bearing his name.[149] Henry Selby did not record a will, and I did not find a court-ordered division of his property following his death in 1898.

Since he was an owner of our property, I looked up Henry S. Selby's U.S. Census records to see what more I could learn about the remainder of his life. In 1860, he owned no slaves, and his occupation was "farmer."[150] This is a surprise. Living at the Wynkoop Tavern his whole life, he was by no means ever a traditional farmer. Since he owned our farm by 1860, the census enumerator might have thought he qualified as a farmer or farm overseer. In the 1870 census, he had reverted to having no occupation—no doubt a different enumerator's interpretation than the one in 1860.[151] The 1880 census reported Henry as unmarried, a lodger, not the head of the household, and again having no occupation.[152]

We know he never married and did not work in the conventional sense, but why was Henry not the head of the household? I checked to see if his older sister, Sally, Colonel Hamtramck's widow, was the head-of-household since she lived in the same house with Henry until her death in 1889. She was not head of the household in 1880 either, but I could not find out who was. According to the U.S. Census Bureau, a 1921 fire at the Commerce Department building in Washington destroyed or severely damaged most of the 1890 census records, including those from West Virginia.[153] Henry died intestate and without children before the 1900 census, so we have seen the last census information about him in 1880.

Much more information, some of it humorous, about Henry Selby's activities—plus those of several other Selby and Hamtramck family members—surfaced late in my research. It comes from the *Spirit of Jefferson*

---

149 West Virginia GeoHistory/Geoexplorer Project, "1883 S. Howell Brown Map," 2010. Retrieved from http://www.wvgeohistory.org/BrowseResources/1883SHowellBrownMapMode

150 1860 U.S. Census, record of Henry S. Selby. Retrieved from http://www.wvgeohistory.org/Search.aspx#v=6733-census-1860

151 1870 U.S. Census, record of Henry S. Selby. Retrieved from http://www.wvgeohistory.org/Search.aspx#v=2532-census-1870

152 1880 U.S. Census, record of Henry S. Selby. Retrieved from http://www.wvgeohistory.org/Search.aspx#v=9512-census-1880

153 Wikipedia contributors, "1890 United States Census." Retrieved from https://en.wikipedia.org/wiki/1890_United_States_Census

and the *Shepherdstown Register* via the Library of Congress's Chronicling America project.

The articles begin in 1873, when we discover that a particular fly nearly ruined all of Henry Selby's and many others' wheat crops. Some farmers planned to plow their wheat under and plant corn, while others turned their livestock out onto the fields.[154] This blow did not seem to discourage Henry. Two years later he bought thirty-five more acres of farmland from Stephen Staley, which were situated directly across Engle Molers Road from Henry's central farm.[155] A few years later the *Shepherdstown Register* reported that Henry Selby had sold the most excellent lot of wheat that season for 93¢ a bushel.[156] This may have been the origin of the name "Wheatland" for his farm, which appears in a 1914 deed and on a 1928 map—discussed shortly under the farm ownership of Eliza Williamson.

An 1888 Chesapeake Fertilizer Company advertisement listed the leading farmers who had used its product the previous season—Henry Selby being one of them. This particular fertilizer consisted mainly of ground bone, guano, and phosphate.[157]

These considerations and others convinced me that Henry actively administered his farm and was not an idle farm landlord as I had thought initially. They also persuaded me to rethink what type of tenants lived at our farmhouse. I now believe the tenants were more like managers hired to oversee farm operations and laborers.

In 1874, Henry Selby and two nieces sold his father's brick storehouse on German Street for $3,000 to James Greenwood (Deed No. 29).[158] Unfortunately, by 1879, some unpaid lien holders on the property took Selby and Greenwood to court to recover amounts not named.[159] Since

---

154 *Shepherdstown Register*, Shepherdstown, W. Va., May 31, 1873, 2. LOC Chronicling America.

155 *Shepherdstown Register*, Shepherdstown, W. Va., July 31, 1875, 2. LOC Chronicling America.

156 *Shepherdstown Register*, Shepherdstown, W. Va., August 24, 1878, 2. LOC Chronicling America.

157 *Shepherdstown Register*, Shepherdstown, W. Va., July 13, 1888, 2. LOC Chronicling America.

158 *Spirit of Jefferson*, Charles Town, W. Va., March 10, 1874, 3. LOC Chronicling America.

159 *Spirit of Jefferson*, Charles Town, W. Va., July 15, 1879, 4. LOC Chronicling America.

the *Spirit of Jefferson* announcement states that the storehouse was built
of brick, I think the question about which of the two possible buildings
it could have been in the photograph in Figure 5.5 is settled. The fifth
building from the intersection of German and Princess Streets was built of
brick, while the fourth building from the same corner was made of stone.
Dr. James Price was right—Selby's store was the brick building. Newer
buildings have replaced both structures.

In an unrelated item the same year, the *Shepherdstown Register* reported
that three sizable men met by chance one day in 1879 at the railroad
station in Shepherdstown. While a farmer was weighing wheat and
loading it on a rail car for Baltimore, the three men took advantage of the
large scale and weighed themselves. Henry Selby was the heaviest at 264
pounds.[160]

A few years later we see another curious story in the same newspaper.
Vincent Dorsey, an African American identified as "colored" in the article,
shot a crane with a wingspan of six feet five inches on Henry Selby's
farm.[161] The crane might have been the bird we know as the great blue
heron—still a frequent visitor to the farm and its pond—sometimes
erroneously called a crane.

A long and laudatory obituary appeared after Henry Selby's death in 1898
in contrast to his father's nearly anonymous one in 1855. It called him one
of Shepherdstown's most respected citizens. He had been sick a long time
and died at his home, not having been out of his room for several years.
According to the article, he suffered greatly, but "with singular patience
and fortitude," was conscious until the end, and retained his faculties
almost intact. The funeral service took place at his home. The article
described Henry as "reserved and retiring . . . who mingled little with
the world," and "although one of the wealthiest men in the community
led a quiet and unostentatious life." It portrayed him as an excellent
businessman who achieved notable success until the very last.

We also learn that he was well informed on current events, and knew the
trend of public affairs. He was born, lived, and died in the same house—

160 *Shepherdstown Register*, Shepherdstown, W. Va., September 27, 1879, 2. LOC
Chronicling America.
161 *Shepherdstown Register*, Shepherdstown, W. Va., October 8, 1881, 2. LOC Chronicling
America.

the Wynkoop Tavern. The article described the house as "[A] solid old colonial mansion of brick such as the early Virginians used to build." He never slept one night away from his own home. Most interesting of all, he was on the jury that tried one of John Brown's co-conspirators, but as a result, had to remain in Charles Town until after midnight. He still walked home—about ten miles—rather than stay away all night.

Two of Henry's pall-bearers' names connect with the farmhouse. William Myers was a recent manager of Henry's farm and John Show was either a son or other relative of an earlier farm manager—George Show. I will introduce the tenant farm managers in Chapter 7.[162]

Mysteriously, Henry is absent from the photo in Figure 5.9, even though he is supposed never to have spent a night away from the house pictured in it. The wording of his obituary may help explain why, since he must have been at the party shown in the photo. His "reserved and retiring" character mentioned in his obit, and perhaps his considerable weight, may have persuaded him to occupy himself elsewhere.

Henry Selby's nieces and nearest relatives, Eliza Williamson and Florence Shepherd—daughters of John F. Hamtramck and his second wife, Eliza Claggett Selby—would inherit our farmhouse from Henry. Helen Boteler Pendleton writes that Florence and Eliza Hamtramck "made the old house [Wynkoop Tavern] a pleasant and hospitable place in their day."[163]

News of Henry Selby did not end with his death. A 1911 story lamented the razing of John H. Snyder's old log blacksmith shop at Princess and Washington Streets. It stated that the shop was more than a workplace. After the covering of fires in the evening, neighborhood "wiseacres" gathered to discuss public affairs. The article recounted how Henry Selby, when living, attended regularly but, true to character, said little himself.[164] Pendleton described him as a stout and heavy-eyed man who sat day-by-day, rain or shine, on the street corner, then called Harris's Corner.[165]

---

162 *Shepherdstown Register*, Shepherdstown, W.Va., April 21, 1898, 3. LOC Chronicling America.
163 Pendleton, 13.
164 *Shepherdstown Register*, Shepherdstown, W.Va., July 27, 1911, 3. LOC Chronicling America.
165 Pendleton, 11.

This spot is the northeast corner of the intersection of German and Princess Streets where the 1906 Yellow Brick Bank building stands today.

Thus ends the nineteenth century and the story of the first two generations of Selbys in Shepherdstown.

The primary reason I have not found much information on the Selby family during the early nineteenth century is that there was not as much newspaper coverage of the area during that period as there was later. The *Potomak Guardian and Berkeley Advertiser* began publication in Shepherdstown in 1790 but moved to Martinsburg a few years later, where its successor ceased publication in 1800. I have already described a few items I found in it among the Berkeley County Historical Society's microfilm archives. The trouble with trying to do research in this publication is that it is not indexed. Therefore, finding relevant material requires scrolling through every issue and glancing over every article.

Another early newspaper was the *Martinsburg Gazette* whose predecessor started in 1826 and whose successor ceased in 1857. Fortunately, the Berkeley County Historical Society has a microfilmed copy of the *Martinsburg Gazette*, which has been manually indexed as I mentioned before under Walter B. Selby's entry. Another microfilm copy of this newspaper is available at the West Virginia University Library.

Charles Town's *Spirit of Jefferson* commenced publication in 1844 and published until 1948, affording a more fruitful source of material for this project than some of the earlier local periodicals. However, the Martinsburg and Charles Town papers did not provide extensive coverage of doings in Shepherdstown. The *Shepherdstown Register* began publication in 1849 and continued until 1955, supplying the most material of any periodical about our story's characters. Unfortunately, both the Charles Town and Shepherdstown papers went dark during the Civil War, depriving us of information about our people during that crucial period.

I have seen several articles in the *Shepherdstown Register* referring to an old weekly called the *American Eagle* published in Shepherdstown from about 1816 to 1819. The Library of Congress website informs us that the Library of Virginia in Richmond is the only repository for the *American Eagle*. It would be interesting to know if it contains any references to our farmhouse, its owner, or residents. The existence of this resource demonstrates that there are practically no limits to the sources I could seek out. But I have drawn the line here and elsewhere—based on my resources and energy—for how far I will go to pursue them.

Florence Shepherd and Eliza Williamson 1898–1914

We now move on to the next owners of the farmhouse. Florence Shepherd and Eliza Williamson inherited it and its land from their uncle, Henry S. Selby. They were the daughters of Eliza Claggett Selby and Colonel John F. Hamtramck and granddaughters of Walter B. Selby. However, there is no public record of a transfer of the property between Henry Selby's 1898 death and 1914 when Florence granted Eliza full title to the farmhouse and 275 acres surrounding it.

Neither woman ever lived in the house. Eliza Williamson moved to Baltimore with her husband after their marriage. Florence Shepherd and her husband, James, lived in Shepherdstown and eventually relocated to the Wynkoop Tavern after Florence's aunt Sally's death in 1889. Since bachelor Henry Selby would then have been its sole remaining occupant besides possible servants, he might have welcomed the company of his niece's family in the sizable house. The two sisters rented or let out the farmhouse to tenants like the previous Selby family owners.

The photograph in Figure 5.10 shows James and Florence Shepherd with their grandson, George Waters Billmyer, seated on the front porch of the Wynkoop Tavern.[166] The grandson was born in 1901, which would date the photo as circa 1903. It shows Florence (about age sixty-seven) and James (about age eighty-two) as a much older couple than in the 1867 picture in Figure 5.9. Even so, they bear striking resemblances to their younger selves.

The only personal details we have about Florence Shepherd come from her 1918 obituary. It recounts how she was stricken with paralysis soon after she arrived at her daughter's in Charles Town where she planned to spend the winter. It tells how she was from one of Shepherdstown's

---

166 Shepherd House, later Elise Billmyer's House, 204 E. German Street, Shepherdstown, W.Va., James Shepherd family seated in front, photograph, early 1900s. Retrieved from http://www.wvgeohistory.org/portals/0/zoomify/URLDrivenPage2 .htm?zImagePath=/portals/0/images/Hist_Shepherdstown_2014_02_032&&zSkinPath =Assets/Skins/Default

most prominent families—well known and highly regarded, a refined and cultured woman of remarkable intelligence and sound judgment. The article reports:

> She was the last of a notable circle of women in that part of town who had for more than half a century been friends and neighbors, and she had felt deeply the loss as one by one they have preceded her to the other shore.

FIGURE 5.10 James and Florence Shepherd with grandson, circa 1903. *Image courtesy of the Historic Shepherdstown Commission.*

She did not profess the Catholic faith of her father and sister Eliza but belonged to the Episcopal Church in town. Finally, the item told that her sister, Eliza, of Baltimore, was the last of their generation.[167]

---

167 *Shepherdstown Register*, Shepherdstown, W.Va., October 10, 1918, 3. LOC Chronicling America.

Eliza Williamson 1914–1921

As of January 8, 1914, Florence Shepherd and Eliza Williamson jointly
owned equal shares of three parcels known as the Cherry Hill, Red Pump,
and Wheatland farms. These properties were about two miles south
of Shepherdstown and contained approximately 596 acres, according
to Deed No. 30. This deed partitions the property between the two
women. Florence Shepherd granted her full title and interest to her sister
Eliza Williamson in that part of the land labeled as Tract No. 1, which
included about 275 acres. A map of this tract accompanies the deed,
which shows that it consists of the farm then known as Wheatland and
our log farmhouse. The 1883 tax map showing Henry S. Selby as owner
establishes a clear line of inheritance for the Wheatland farm from Walter
B. Selby to these two granddaughters through his son, Henry.

A 1928 map drawn by Shaw and Whitmer identifies the farmhouse's
property as Wheatland.[168] This is the first appearance of Wheatland on a
published map. The farm may have acquired this name around 1873 when
the *Shepherdstown Register* reported on the bumper wheat crop Henry Selby
harvested on his farm, as previously noted under his entry.

The 1928 map also shows the Red Pump and Cherry Hill farmhouses. The
Red Pump farmhouse appears along Shepherdstown Pike a short distance
north of a fork between it and Flowing Spring Road. The 1852 tax map
shows that this house was on Walter Selby's farmland. Today the house
is gone, but there is a cluster of trees, rusted machinery, and corrugated
metal roofing at the site.

The Cherry Hill farmhouse appears to the east of present-day Morgan
Grove Road a little north of its intersection with Gardners Lane on
the 1928 map. The 1852 tax map shows this house on Colonel John F.
Hamtramck's land. Since Colonel Hamtramck married into the Selby
family, the Cherry Hill part of the 596-acre tract must have gone to his
daughters Florence Shepherd and Eliza Williamson after his 1858 death. If
this house were still standing, it would be on private property and too far
off the road to be visible. The Jefferson County assessor's office website
now shows this property to be a 205-acre tract described as Cherry Hill,

---

168 Shaw and Whitmer, "Map of Jefferson County West Virginia," 1928. Retrieved from
http://www.wvgeohistory.org

but it lists no house or year built.[169] Likewise, the Jefferson County Historic Landmarks Commission map shows nothing on this tract, indicating that this house too is gone.

We learn a few things about Eliza Hamtramck Williamson from local newspapers. In 1866—before she had married—the town appointed a ladies' committee to arrange memorial services to honor the Confederate dead. Eliza was part of the floral committee selected "to collect flowers to be scattered as affectionate tributes over the last resting place of the lost ones."[170]

The *Shepherdstown Register* notes in 1880 that Eliza "has a situation in the Treasury Department, Washington, as clerk."[171] Her husband, Luke Williamson, died the previous year. She may have had to work if her husband did not leave sufficient income for her. Relatively few women participated in the workforce in 1880, so it would have stood out for a forty-one-year-old widow to secure a government job. As the daughter of Colonel John F. Hamtramck, Eliza may have been able to use his reputation and contacts to her gain.

Relocating to Washington must not have been easy. I encountered no other family members living there. Finally, we learn that Eliza "and her two charming daughters," Florence and Gay Selby of Baltimore, were spending the summer of 1889 with her sister, Florence Shepherd, at the Wynkoop Tavern.[172] Florence and husband James had moved into the tavern as already noted after her aunt, Sally Selby Hamtramck, died at the house in May of 1889.[173] Evidently, by age fifty Eliza no longer needed paid employment and had moved back to Baltimore. I did not find a record of when she died.

169 Jefferson County, West Virginia Assessor's Office, "GIS Map," 2015. Retrieved from http://jefferson.wvassessor.com/Maps/GIS-Map

170 *Spirit of Jefferson*, Charles Town, W. Va., June 19, 1866, 2. LOC Chronicling America.

171 *Shepherdstown Register*, Shepherdstown, W. Va , May 22, 1880, 2. LOC Chronicling America.

172 *Shepherdstown Register*, Shepherdstown, W. Va., July 12, 1889, 3. LOC Chronicling America.

173 *Shepherdstown Register*, Shepherdstown, W. Va., May 31, 1889, 2. LOC Chronicling America.

Florence Williamson Sampson and Gay Selby Williamson 1921–1930

The next owners of our farmhouse received it from their mother, Eliza Williamson. On April 5, 1921, Eliza granted her daughters, Florence Williamson Sampson and Gay Selby Williamson, a parcel of real estate about two miles south of Shepherdstown known as Wheatland farm having about 275 acres including its farmhouse. Neither of these sisters ever lived in the house. Gay Selby died in Baltimore in 1930 where her mother had moved many years earlier after marrying Luke Tiernan Williamson.

Later owners, Mark Mulligan and David Haarberg, informed us that the two-story wood-frame west wing of the log farmhouse dates from 1929, which falls within the period of Florence's and Gay's ownership. Mulligan and Haarberg learned this fact from owner Gilbert Wright who sold the property to them. This wing is a substantial addition. It is difficult to believe absentee owners built it for tenants. I will offer more information about this addition in ensuing chapters.

Florence Williamson Sampson 1930–1946

Upon her death in 1930, Gay Selby Williamson left the Hamtramck silver and three commissions of her great-grandfather, Jean-François Hamtramck, to her sister, Florence Williamson Sampson—later to become Florence W. Clarke—as well as all the rest of her estate including her share of the log farmhouse property. Gay also left $1,000 to the Woman's Library—today the Shepherdstown Library—and $1,000 to St. Agnes Catholic Church of Shepherdstown. These last two bequests stand out since Gay likely never lived in Shepherdstown, although they do speak of her family's strong connection to it.

Final Notes

I made several attempts to locate Selby family members who might still be in the Shepherdstown vicinity to see if they had any records, stories, or memories of their ancestors. The local 2016 telephone directory lists three Selbys. Since Walter B. Selby's descendants owned our farmhouse until 1946, I hoped that one of the listed Selbys might recall stories they had heard about it directly from older relatives. I contacted each of them. Although one of these Selbys was from Maryland, as was Walter B. Selby, his family had moved to West Virginia much later, and he knew nothing of the nineteenth-century Selbys. The other two local Selbys also knew nothing about Walter B. Selby or his descendants. I conclude that Walter Selby's descendants may not be readily traceable due to the obscuring of the Selby surname through marriage. Only Walter Selby's daughters produced offspring thus complicating the tracing of his heirs.

Elise Shepherd Billmyer, Florence Shepherd's granddaughter, still owned the Wynkoop Tavern until her death in 1985, after which it passed out of Selby hands—a total of 175 years in the same family.[174] Several Billmyers still live in the area; however, after some attempts I did not succeed in contacting any of them.

Thus, I have unearthed what I could from public records, local histories, and periodicals about the early owners of our log farmhouse and property. Still, I feel I know too little about these people. There is no telling what biases, distortions, and unevenness the particular documents I have used introduce into their lives. The next chapter will add more personal details about some of the Selbys and Hamtramcks than I have captured in this chapter, helping us fill out the stories of their lives a bit more.

These personal details come from the John Francis Hamtramck Papers. I discovered these papers only through repeated internet searches on our characters' first names, surnames, and their combinations and variations. I hope that more personal papers of the pioneering Morgans, Selbys, and Hamtramcks may emerge, possibly because of this manuscript reaching someone with knowledge of them. Conceivably, more personal material from these early families may find its way onto the ever-expanding internet and catch our attention as the Hamtramck Papers did mine.

---

174 Jefferson County Clerk, *Deed Book 935*, Page 11, February 8, 2000.

CHAPTER 6 HAMTRAMCK PAPERS

COLONEL JOHN F. HAMTRAMCK'S personal papers, held by Duke University's David M. Rubenstein Rare Book and Manuscript Library, proved to be a windfall to my research. The collection, termed the "John Francis Hamtramck Papers, 1757–1862," includes letters to John Francis Hamtramck and his father-in-law, Walter B. Selby, from some of their children and others. It contains many other materials, such as military papers, and documents relating to the Osage Indian Nation. For brevity, I will refer to this collection as the JFH Papers.

The Rubenstein Library purchased this collection in five installments between 1948 and 1972. A staff person told me that dealers sold the records to the Library. Shepherd University Library staff indicated the Rubenstein Library might have bought some of its other Shepherdstown collections of personal papers directly from the families.

Once I had located the JFH papers I had to see them. At last, I had found a resource that contained personal correspondence of people associated with our farmhouse. Lynne and I traveled to Durham, North Carolina, and spent two days perusing nearly all 2,630 items in the collection. These are primary sources—mostly handwritten—which made us feel as if nothing stood between the writers and us, except for the fragile papers in our hands.

Throughout this chapter, I will present the most interesting material I found in the JFH Papers. Unfortunately, these documents bore no references to our farmhouse or its occupants even though John F. Hamtramck was the son-in-law of one owner, father of two other owners, and grandfather of two more owners of the house and farm. Nevertheless, some of the letters do afford glimpses into the daily lives, mundane cares, strengths, and shortcomings of their Selby and Hamtramck family authors. None of the owners of our house wrote any of the letters in the collection, although some of their sisters did.

This chapter includes documents primarily from the JFH Papers; however, I have added some from other sources. I chose the latter archives because they tie into related JFH Papers material more closely than with other texts about their authors or recipients elsewhere in this story. The items I present are in roughly chronological order.

Some of the JFH Papers material was in French from a merchant who sold supplies to John F. Hamtramck for the Osage Indians. Some of the letters were in Spanish from writers dealing with Colonel Hamtramck during the American military occupation of Mexico between 1846 and 1848. I did not attempt to translate any of these letters as they were too peripheral to this study.

Contrary to customary guidance opposed to using long direct quotes from source materials, in many cases, I have done the opposite. My reasons are that quotes from the JFH Papers are uniquely personal, written in polite nineteenth-century voices, and have never been published before to my knowledge. They put the reader in direct touch with historical figures, their colorful language, their excellent qualities, and at times their pettiness. I could not do justice by paraphrasing them all, nor would the reader get an authentic impression of the writers' personalities or states of mind.

John Francis Hamtramck, the central figure of the JFH Papers, whose portrait appears in Figure 6.1, is of great local and national interest.[175] Although he held the ranks of Captain, Major, and ultimately Colonel, I will usually refer to him as Colonel for simplicity. His paternal grandmother was from Quebec, Canada, and his grandfather from Luxembourg. His like-named French-Canadian father, Jean-François Hamtramck (1757–1803), joined the American forces during the Revolutionary War. He was prominent in posts around Detroit, which he captured when intelligence turned up that the British were soon to withdraw from their American placements.[176]

Now for a trivia moment. The City of Hamtramck, Michigan—named for Jean-François Hamtramck—was in the news in 2015 for being the first majority-Muslim city in America.[177]

John F. Hamtramck was born in 1798 in Fort Wayne, Indiana, to Jean-François Hamtramck and his second wife, Rebecca McKenzie Hamtramck (1775–1851). Jean-François's first wife, Marie Joseph Edeline, died in

---

175 West Virginia Division of Culture and History, "On this Day in West Virginia History." Retrieved from http://www.wvculture.org/history/thisdayinwvhistory/1118.html
176 Pendleton, 12.
177 Bailey, Sarah Pulliam, "In the first majority-Muslim U.S. city, residents tense about its future," *The Washington Post*, November 21, 2015.

1796.[178] John F. Hamtramck was five years old when his father died in 1803. Afterward, he became the ward of the future ninth president of the United States, William Henry Harrison. I believe this plan meant that Harrison became the boy's protector after his father's death, not his foster or adoptive parent since his mother was still living. Harrison was then serving as the first congressional delegate from the Northwest Territories.[179] John F. Hamtramck graduated from West Point in 1819. Today his West Point diploma hangs in the Historic Shepherdstown Museum. Later in his career, he served as U.S. Indian agent for the Osage Nation in St. Louis from May 1826 to July 1830.[180]

FIGURE 6.1 Colonel John Francis Hamtramck. *Image courtesy of West Virginia State Archives.*

Helen Boteler Pendleton tells us that John F. Hamtramck's first wife was a Miss Williamson of Maryland and that they had two small daughters, Julia and Mary.[181] The Hamtramck family tree noted in the previous chapter elaborates on and contradicts some of Pendleton's material. It reveals Hamtramck's first wife's name was Marie Antoinette Williamson, born 1801 and died 1822. It also identifies her as the daughter of D. Williamson Esq. and Mary Julianne of Baltimore. However, it characterizes Julia as Hamtramck's granddaughter—his daughter Mary

178 Historic Shepherdstown & Museum, "Hamtramck Family Tree," Selby Family Folder.

179 Wikipedia contributors, "William Henry Harrison." Retrieved from https://en.wikipedia.org/wiki/William_Henry_Harrison

180 Historic Shepherdstown & Museum, "John Francis Hamtramck biography." Retrieved from http://historicshepherdstown.com/portfolio-item/john-francis-hamtramck/

181 Pendleton, 12.

Rebecca's child. The family tree gives Colonel Hamtramck's daughter Mary Rebecca's dates as 1822–1852, which raises the question of whether his first wife, Marie Antoinette, might have died in childbirth.

Early Letters 1825–1827

Continuing the subject of slavery in Walter Selby's life already mentioned in the previous chapter, I found an 1825 letter among the JFH Papers that Walter Selby received from a James Randall of Clarksburg, Virginia. Randall urges Walter Selby to attend a sale of some slaves. In the letter, Randall was anxious that some of the slaves might flee, but a Mr. Israel assured him there was no danger of their running away.[182] I do not know who owned these slaves but, clearly, Walter Selby was involved in trafficking them. Slave trading was documented by deeds in the same way as real estate contracts. I found an 1832 deed (No. 22) that named Walter Selby as a grantee for the purchase of four slaves—Harry, Aley, Thornton, and Ann. I did not research Walter Selby's grantor deeds either for land or slaves; however, this would be an interesting topic for further research.

One aspect of slavery in Jefferson County was that its slave population amounted to over twenty-eight percent of the county's 1860 census population of 14,052—the highest percentage of any of the counties that were to become part of West Virginia.[183] Jefferson County's many slaves might have been a mark of greater prosperity in the county, relative to the other counties, achieved partly at the cost of involuntary labor.

We turn next to John F. Hamtramck, who as a young widower came to a ball in Shepherdstown at the Wynkoop Tavern in 1825 where he met and fell in love with Walter Selby's oldest daughter, Eliza Claggett Selby. The ball undoubtedly took place in the two connected rooms that I described earlier, which Lynne and I visited in person. They married that year and went on to have six children, three of whom died in infancy between 1832 and 1836, and only two of whom survived to maturity.[184] These two

---

182 Randall, James, letter to Walter B. Selby, July 22, 1825, John Francis Hamtramck Papers, David M. Rubenstein Rare Book & Manuscript Library, Duke University (hereafter cited as JFH Papers).

183 Graham, Henry S., "Map of Virginia: showing the distribution of its slave population from the census of 1860," Library of Congress. Retrieved from http://www.loc.gov/resource/g3881e.cw1047000/

184 Historic Shepherdstown & Museum, Selby family folder, "Descendants of Walter Bowie Selby," 2.

children were Florence and Eliza (Sarah Frances) who came to jointly own our log farmhouse after their uncle Henry Selby's death.

Several letters to Colonel Hamtramck among the JFH Papers commend him on his marriage to Eliza Claggett Selby. A cousin, Emily Markland, tells him she learned about the wedding through an already-invited intimate friend. She confesses surprise that he had not mentioned a word of it in his recent letter. She informs, a bit sarcastically, that she is interested to hear everything that concerns him if he can spare sufficient time from his dearly beloved. She ends by expressing her hope that his engagement will lead to a happy union.[185]

Elias Kent Kane, a U.S. Senator from Illinois, wrote from the senate chamber in Washington in 1826 to congratulate Hamtramck on his fortunate marriage. He says that Jane, whom I assume to be Kane's wife, speaks loudly in praise of Hamtramck's better half, and refers to Hamtramck's own description of his wife as "an inestimable treasure," in a recent letter.[186] Another correspondent from Washington, Walter Laurie, says he has heard that Eliza Selby Hamtramck is one of the most accomplished and amiable of her sex. Laurie goes on to say he considers Hamtramck's appointment assured but does not mention to what office.[187]

In December 1827, Hamtramck received a letter in St. Louis from D. Williamson (Mary Rebecca's grandfather) in Baltimore. Hamtramck's daughter Mary Rebecca lives with her maternal grandparents who oversee her education. There is no record to tell us why Mary was not in her father's care at this time—perhaps it was to spare her the anticipated deprivations of living on the frontier with her father during his tenure as Indian agent for the Osage Nation. Or, Colonel Hamtramck's new wife might not have welcomed having to raise his first wife's daughter.

Mary's grandfather describes her as skilled at school, healthy, and intelligent. He writes that fifty dollars a year is enough for Mary's clothing and education. He also relates that Mary and her grandmother have "their little spats," but "in general live in the greatest possible friendship."

---

185 Markland, Emily, letter to John Francis Hamtramck, September 11, 1825. JFH Papers.
186 Kane, Elias Kent, letter to John Francis Hamtramck, January 11, 1826. JFH Papers.
187 Laurie, Walter, letter to John Francis Hamtramck, January 30, 1826. JFH Papers.

D. Williamson goes on to write that he is "descending the path of age to grave," and to congratulate Hamtramck on his first child with second wife, Eliza.[188] This child would be Ellen Eliza who was born in 1827. I discovered an inconsistent detail in Ellen Eliza's 1847 death notice—that she was eighteen at death.[189] However, I am convinced of her 1827 birth year, which is corroborated by the Hamtramck family tree noted in the previous chapter. Furthermore, Ellen Eliza's letters from the JFH Papers dated in the late 1830's reveal a more mature child than one born in 1829 would have been.

Indian Agent for the Osage Nation

It is clear that John Francis Hamtramck's appointment mentioned in Walter Laurie's letter was to the post of Indian agent for the Osage Nation. President John Quincy Adams decreed his commissioning to this office on May 2, 1826.[190] General William Clark, Superintendent of Indian Affairs in St. Louis, sent a letter to Hamtramck soon after his appointment issuing instructions to move to his post to settle some tribal disputes. It is so fascinating that I quote it in its entirety here. The spelling, grammar, and punctuation are not always correct by current standards, but I have preserved them for historical accuracy for this and other letters that I present from the JFH Papers. The only thing I have changed to improve readability is to insert paragraph breaks where there are usually none or too few in the original. General Clark writes:

> Superintendency Ind. Affs.   July 7th 1826
> John F. Hamtramck Esq Sir
>
> It will be necessary for you to be at the post assigned to the Osage Agent. In time to meet that nation on their return from their Summer hunt; and in Council make it known to the Osages that the "Delawares" complain that the Osages have killed 11 of their people & taken many horses, & more than 600 skins etc, and that they had retaliated & killed 8 or 10 Osages, and had determined to carry on a war against them joined by other Tribes. State to them, that certain unsettled differences yet exist between

---

188 Williamson, D., letter to John Francis Hamtramck, December 10, 1827. JFH Papers.

189 *Martinsburg Gazette*, Martinsburg, Va., June 25, 1847, 3. BCHS microfilm archives.

190 Adams, John Quincy, appointment of John Francis Hamtramck as Indian Agent to the Osage Indians, May 2, 1826. Retrieved from https://www.invaluable.co.uk/auction-lot/adams,-john-quincy.-document -signed,-j.q.-adams,-211-c-2a34833a48

them & the Cherokees, which was not settled at their last meeting. State that it is the work of the President & it is also my desire, that a settlement of all differences between those Tribes, placed under my Superintendency should take place as soon as possible to enable us to make an attempt to better their situation.

You will State to the Osages, that they having expressed by their Sub Agent a wish to meet the Delawares at this place for the purpose of explanation & adjustment of existing difficulties, which has been communicated to the Delawares by their Agent Maj. Graham, and the Delawares have agreed to meet the Osages at St. Louis the 15th of September next, and have sent to the Cherokees, to send a deputation to meet them & the Indians at that time.

State to them the necessity of their being prompt & decisive in what they wish & intend to do in these serious accusations. It will be necessary for them to select from the several Towns, proper men to represent the Nation in all matters, composed of Chief, Braves considerate men & warriors, and send to this place for the purposes before stated. & if they have been the aggressors, peace cannot be affected, but by a compliance of what is just right.

You will accompany the delegation of Osages through the settlements to this place, & furnish them in passing our settlements with some beef and corn or bread, to a moderate amount for which you will keep regular receipts.

It is expected that the delegation will not exceed in all forty persons. After consulting with the Osages & becoming acquainted with their intentions, you will please to send an express to me stating the report of their decision and give all information of importance, particularly in relation to the present contest.

The persons employed in the agency, to which you have been appointed, and Paul L. Cho[u]teau [who succeeded Hamtramck as Osage Indian Agent], . . . Paul Louise interp. for the nation, Agnt Cho[u]teau interpreter at Cantonment Gibson [in Oklahoma], R. Dunlap Black & Gen. Smith & another Smith will be employed when the Indians commence their permanent Settlements.

Payments have been made to the Sub. Agent and hired men for the 3rd quarter of the present year, from that time, you will commence the payments & settle the accounts of your agency, as required by your Instructions.

The amount due to the Osages on account of annuities this year having been paid to them by their late agent in merchandise to the amount $4,677, and the balance of $3,820 being deducted for spoliations, you will only explain the nature of these claims, on which deduction has been made and procure receipts for the $8,500 annuity.

Respectfully Sir
Yr Obt Sevt, Wm Clark[191]

John F. Hamtramck's young wife, Eliza, wrote a letter to her father, Walter Selby, in July 1826 from Cincinnati. Here is her message in which she scoldingly writes:

Cincinnati   July 30th 1826
My Dear Father,

I received your last letter and most [of] the contents I cannot perfectly comprehend what you mean when you say you have not consulted your wishes in regard to the furniture sent as nothing has been sent on but some glass and tea china [and] a cooking glass.

You are well aware the servants have been made over to me and in case of my death to Henry and Sally. What more you could desire from Maj. Hamtramck I cannot imagine.

I think my husband has acted a generous part by me, more so than many husbands would. We both stand a good chance to his long life time and it depends much upon you to make it a happy one. I spend many a sleepless night thinking of my situation as I have been made an outcast and for what, God only knows.

You do not know Mr. Hamtramck's disposition as well as I do or you would not tamper with it for my sake. He is affectionate and very fond of me but he cannot bear to be crossed. . . . You surely cannot think your withholding the furniture honorable when you have made it over to us or rather given Mr. Hamtramck a bill of sale for it. You surely cannot forget that.

Let not my ill health be any longer a plea for not sending it. . . . [M]y husband . . . has procured a house for us as we intend going to housekeeping in September. . . . Boarding is too expensive. We cannot afford it any longer. We paid $40 for staying a week at Lexington and our expenses here are very great—too much so for our house which is a small one. . . . If you for a moment knew how miserable you have made me by having opened our furniture you would require no other inducement to send it. . . . Your heart would bleed for me.

Am I not your child and have I not a claim to your affection? I am in a strange land with no friend or relation but my husband. If he is not kind to me to whom can I look. . . . My piano can be of no use to anyone at home nor yet my music books. My drawings can give no one pleasure there. . . . Many tedious hours have I spent over those paintings and now

---

191 Clark, General William, letter to John Francis Hamtramck, July 7, 1826. JFH Papers.

they are taken from me. . . . Hours have I dedicated to my piano when my school companions were playing and now my piano is taken from me.

Great God it is too much for me to bear. I cannot bear it. . . . Do not talk of my ever returning to your house for God's sake. . . . I have been born to persecutions and to sorrow. . . . [F]or the last time I implore you as you value my happiness to send on my furniture. . . . Pray to Almighty God your next letter may announce our furniture's being packed up. . . . I wish my letters to be postpaid as I have no money. . . . You have heard from me for the last time. . . . My determination is fixed and irrevocable.

E. Hamtramck[192]

One could feel sorry for Walter Selby after this display of ingratitude, or instead, think him an uncaring parent. However, the letters in the JFH Papers only reveal one side of exchanges between correspondents. It includes posts to but not from Walter Selby, as is the case with all the other letter recipients represented in the collection. Hence, I will reserve judgment without his side of the story.

This letter indicates John and Eliza Hamtramck might have stayed in Cincinnati for a time before moving on to their post in St. Louis. Since Lexington is far to the north of Cincinnati, it might have been an earlier way station on route to St. Louis. Let us hope they eventually received their furniture and the servants. The writers of these personal letters rarely referred to their servants as slaves, although slaves they indeed were. Some quarters of society might have considered it too indelicate a term even in the antebellum South.

Eliza mentions her younger brother and sister, Henry and Sally, in her letter to whom their father promised the servants in case of her death. I could not learn why Eliza's other living siblings were not guaranteed any servants but suspect they had been promised other things. After all, there would not have been enough servants to promise one to every sibling.

Walter Selby's youngest daughter, Sarah Ellen (Sally), writes a letter to him in 1829 while staying in St. Louis visiting her sister Eliza and her brother-in-law, John F. Hamtramck. Although not reproachful like Eliza's 1826 letter, it appeals for money but in a persuasive style. She pleads:

---

192 Hamtramck, Eliza C., letter to Walter B. Selby, July 30, 1826. JFH Papers.

St. Louis   April 29, 1829

My dear Father, I would not reproach you being sick not nearly as practiced in writing as you were formerly. I am sure I seem to have neglected you. . . . You no doubt have heard that Mr. Hamtramck has been removed from office. He will engage in business in this place. General Jackson is making great havoc in the United States. . . . I hope that you have determined to visit this Country. Do, my dearest Papa come out. I know you will be pleased with it. Walter ought to visit St. Louis.

There have been several late arrivals of belles within the last few weeks. . . . A young lady must dress well, or not be admired. . . . [I]t is absolutely necessary to have more clothes than I have. I have had at the rate of fifty dollars a year and that is not sufficient to dress me. The young ladies here dress elegantly and it is a great deal thought of. I never should request money if I did not really want it. I cannot go into company unless I dress handsomely. If I do not dress I cannot expect to be admired.

I am endeavoring to captivate a rich merchant. If I succeed, I shall not be of one cents further expense. I want shoes badly. I have been wearing one pair constantly for six or eight months—gloves the same length of time. I must have one or two summer dresses. I can't do without them. Pa dearest Papa grant my request. You know best what sum will be convenient for you to send. I should like to have forty dollars. . . . You may think I am extravagant, but rest assured it is not so. I wish you could see some of our ladies here. You would be astonished, they are as fashionable as you see in cities. Some of the girls are beautiful. . . . The Indians are very much opposed to Mr. Hamtramck's removal. They say that they will not have any other Agent. Seven or eight of them were here this morning, the principal men of the nation.

How is Henry? I should dearly like to see him and more. . . . Papa do not suffer yourself to be depressed. Cheer up and be happy. When you write me give me all the news. How are Aunt Morgan's family? . . . Hamtramcks constantly arriving and departing. I love dearly to see them coming up. They present a genial appearance. . . . [T]his is the loveliest country I ever seen. I wish you were here to enjoy it. I must now conclude by begging you to write me. Mr. Hamtramck and Eliza join in love to you and family.

Unalterably Your Affectionate
Daughter Sally E. Selby[193]

General Jackson in Sally's message must be the recently inaugurated President Andrew Jackson. She also refers to some family members— Walter, an older brother who would die in 1839, Henry, a younger

---

193 Selby, Sally E., letter to Walter B. Selby, April 29, 1829. JFH Papers.

brother who would inherit our farmhouse from his father, and Aunt Morgan, probably one of Walter Selby's deceased wife's sisters.

Sally kept an undated autograph and sketchbook. She drew a pencil sketch of an Osage Indian and papoose on one of the pages and signed it "by Sally."[194] She must have drafted it in 1829 or 1830 when she was seventeen or eighteen and visiting her sister in St. Louis. The fountain-like plumage in her sketch looks remarkably like that in George Catlin's depictions of Osage Indians painted a few years later. George Catlin specialized in portraits of Native Americans in the 1830's. He was the first European-American to illustrate Plains Indians in their native lands. Sally's sketch appears in Figure 6.2. There might have been an artistic quality in the Selby family if we consider

FIGURE 6.2 Sketch by Sally Selby, circa 1830. *Image courtesy of John F. Hamtramck Papers, David M. Rubenstein Rare Book & Manuscript Library, Duke University.*

Sally's sister Eliza's drawings and paintings mentioned in her 1826 letter.

Elias Kent Kane wrote an interesting letter in 1830, to a Mr. Thomas about John F. Hamtramck's alleged removal from office. He writes:

> Washington   April 18th 1830
> Dear Sir
>
> I was extremely sorry to learn on going to the War Dept. a few days ago, that Francis had been removed from his office of Indian Agent. The reason assigned for it was that the Osages were in a warlike humour & it had become necessary to send amongst them a man of decisive influence to prevent trouble & bloodshed. This will be an unexpected & severe stroke to the poor fellow.
>
> The city of Washington is full of office hunters from Missouri, but whether they have joined in a request for this removal I know not.

---

194 Selby, Sally E., autograph and sketch book, undated. JFH Papers.

Nothing has happened during the winter to give me more pain—upon matters generally, things look very well. I believe opposition to Gen. Jackson from a particular quarter has been abandoned, if the idea was ever seriously entertained. Present my compliments to Mrs. Thomas & believe me

truly yr friend   E K Kane[195]

John F. Hamtramck's status as an Indian agent is confusing. Even though we have Sally Selby's and Elias Kane's letters implying his removal from office, many other documents among the JFH Papers indicate he was still conducting business as Indian agent for the Osages after the dates of those letters. An article on the *historicshepherdstown.com* website states that Hamtramck remained as the Indian agent for the Osage Nation until July 1830. I present information from an article further on in this chapter claiming President Jackson did remove him; however, I believe this question is still an open one based on evidence in the JFH Papers.

Remarkably, the JFH Papers include an undated seven-page Osage–English word list in John F. Hamtramck's own hand. I found virtually no link, however, between the Osage words and their English counterparts in his transcription and those I found through internet searches, except for the names of a few body parts. The existence of this list supports a commendable seriousness with which Hamtramck conducted his duties as Indian agent—in contrast to the poor reputation of many agents.[196]

The word list's most arresting feature is a one-page inventory of religious terms. Besides the Osage and English words in Hamtramck's hand on this page, another unidentified writer penned his understanding of their meaning to the Osage. The unknown writer's attempts to focus on Osage words for *God*, *priest*, and *soul* must have been frustrating. He says the Osage have no exact interpretation corresponding to a western idea of *God*. He states that *priest* is the same as a conjurer to the Osage, who had contact with Catholic priests. He writes that the Osage have no word meaning *soul*, but adds that their sensual lives color their idea of futurity. He alleges that the concept of *soul* fits loosely with Osage belief that a short time after death the body of the deceased will go to the "Town of the Dead."[197]

---

195 Kane, Elias Kent, letter to Mr. Thomas, April 18, 1830. JFH Papers.

196 Wishart, David J., Encyclopedia of the Great Plains, "Indian Agents." Retrieved from http://plainshumanities.unl.edu/encyclopedia/doc/egp.pg.032

197 Unidentified writer, List of Osage–English words, undated. JFH Papers.

Return to Shepherdstown from St. Louis

Before continuing with more letters, for the sake of imposing a measure of chronological order to JFH Papers material, I turn to an 1834 invitation. A committee summoned John F. Hamtramck to attend a ceremony for Major General Marquis de Lafayette who died in Paris on May 20, 1834. The request announces:

> Williamsport   August 26th 1834
> Captain Hamtramck
> Dear Sir,
>
> We the undersigned being duly appointed a committee on the present occasion do respectfully invite yourself, officers and men under your command to join us on the 12th September in offering funeral honors to our illustrious and much to be lamented Lafayette.
>
> Respectfully yours
> Jacob Wolf
> Issac Allen
> Wm. Towson
> Samuel Cunningham
>
> P.S. Please let us hear from you, by an early mail.[198]

Hamtramck received this petition in Shepherdstown where his ledgers show that he was in private business at the time. The Williamsport where this letter originated is likely the nearby Maryland city of the same name. The men under his command would have been the volunteers in the militias he had organized in Shepherdstown.

It looks as if Walter Selby and his son-in-law had reached a business arrangement with each other no later than 1833. Selby might even have turned his dry goods business over to Colonel Hamtramck. The JFH Papers include two ponderous bound volumes of Hamtramck's business accounts. The Rubenstein Library cataloged the first as "John Francis Hamtramck, Jr., Journal 1833–1835."[199] It contains entries for purchases by many townspeople, including Walter B. Selby. Sales were for items such as dress handkerchiefs, white satin slippers, spool cotton, coffee, sugar, soup plates, toothbrushes, buttons, French muslin, molasses, gloves, calico, vests, socks, shaving soap, buckskin shoes, palm hats, thread, combs, and hairbrushes. This was a dry goods business for sure.

---

198 Wolf, Jacob, et al., letter to John Francis Hamtramck, August 26, 1834. JFH Papers.
199 Hamtramck, John F., Journal, 1833–1835. JFH Papers.

The second volume, cataloged as "John Francis Hamtramck, Jr., Ledger, 1835–1837," consists of pages of individual accounts, including one for Walter B. Selby. Selby's account lists only "generic goods," cash, and monies paid to or received from other customers. Daniel Entler's account also includes generic goods, as well as window glass, and many gallons of wine and brandy.[200] The beverages were doubtless for the Entler Hotel.

In 1835, Mary Rebecca Hamtramck had gone away to school and wrote to her father from Georgetown, in Washington, D.C., where she was at the Academy of the Visitation. She writes to her father about Archbishop Eccleston confirming her, about her grandmother's visit, and her hope that he will come to an exhibition at the school in July. Mary's stepsister, Ellen Eliza, writes a note at the end of this letter imploring Mary to visit her in Shepherdstown and suggesting she "can practice Ma's piano, ride out in the carriage, write and read in Pa's office & we will spend our time so pleasantly."[201]

This added note indicates Ellen Eliza lives with her parents who had moved back to Shepherdstown after leaving St. Louis. She must have intended for her father to send this note back to Mary with his next letter. We should not confuse Ellen Eliza with her younger sister, Eliza Hamtramck, who was born to John Hamtramck's second wife, Eliza Claggett Selby in 1839—substantiated by the 1850 U.S. Census. "Ma" in this letter would be Eliza Claggett Selby Hamtramck, and it sounds like she recovered the piano her father failed to send her in 1826 out in Cincinnati. Three years later in 1838, Colonel Hamtramck received an alarming letter in Shepherdstown from Ch. A. Williamson, Mary's uncle and son of her Baltimore grandparents. Here is the message:

Baltimore   Nov 24 1838
J. F. Hamtramck Esq
Dear Sir

It is unfortunate that your daughter should have been the cause to her [Mary's grandmother] of any uneasiness and pain after the more than a mother's care and the only alternative left her, was for the sake of all parties, to restore her to her natural guardian, leaving it entirely with him to dispose of her as might best suit his own views and feelings. . . .

---

200 Hamtramck, John F., Ledger, 1835–1837. JFH Papers.
201 Hamtramck, Ellen Eliza, letter to John Francis Hamtramck, June 15, 1835. JFH Papers.

[T]here was and is no disposition to thrust her off upon anyone—you are the father and my mother has sent her to you. . . . Whilst Mary was under her charge no expense or trouble was spared to make her in every respect, what everyone . . . was desirous she should be, my mother cannot nor will not blame herself, betide Mary what may. . . . You will recollect that in taking charge of Mary mother has always reserved to herself the privilege of returning her to you—It was her intention to have provided for Mary and since the death of my father [D. Williamson] she has used every economy to that single purpose, . . . and now to be disappointed in Mary is truly painful to her—

She therefore now gives her up entirely to you, . . . with a positive determination of not again taking charge of her. . . . She will certainly not upbraid herself for want of the Natural feelings of an adopted mother, and as you fear her example to those you have to bring up, it is of no concern of hers. . . . Always hoping that you as her father will feel yourself bound by the ties of Nature, to cause her so to conduct herself as to be to you a source of comfort and pleasure. . . . I write only at the request of my mother and for the only purpose of saying that Mary is now and will hereafter remain under your charge and responsibility. Her grandmother having found that all her centered hopes of happiness have been completely frustrated and she now hopes and prays that Mary may be a source of more pleasure to you, than she has proven to be for her.

Yrs Very Respectfully
Ch. A. Williamson[202]

Truly damning. Colonel Hamtramck must have sent Mary back to Baltimore after she left the Academy of the Visitation to resume living with her by-then widowed grandmother. I do not know if she had finished her schooling, dropped out, or had to depart for other reasons. Mary might have had to leave school because of problems like those Ch. A. Williamson implies in his letter. Perhaps she was acting out about her father having declined to raise her. Recall D. Williamson's 1827 letter to Mary's father foreshadowing problems between her and her grandmother. I wish Ch. A. Williamson could have written more directly about the appalling behavior Mary exhibited to incite such rejection by her grandmother.

We have an 1839 letter from Ellen Eliza to her father in Shepherdstown soon after she went away to school in Frederick, Maryland. She writes:

---

202 Williamson, Ch. A., letter to John Francis Hamtramck, November 24, 1838. JFH Papers.

Arcadia   4/28/1839
Dear Father

I have been expecting a letter from you Dear Father for two or three days and have not received any, but I promised to write first. I am very much pleased with my situation. It is a delightful place indeed. I went to confession on Saturday, and was at the Sisters the same day. I suppose you have got a bonnet for Folly. When you write do tell what kind of a one it is.

Virginia Taylor is going to make her first communion and when I learn my Catechism I will also be allowed to make mine. Rev. Mr. Kroes will prepare me for it. Tell Aunt Sally I want a black veil. My chapel one is all dirty and has become a very ugly colour from my wearing it in the sun. Do send it the first opportunity. I cannot do without it. My face tans so easily and I go to town every Sunday and sometime on Saturday.

Tell Aunt Sally that I would write to her, but I have nothing to say and I suppose my love will be enough. Kiss dear little Folly and Sarah Frances. Give my love to mammy Celia and all the coloured persons. Excuse my short letter Father as I have nothing more to say. Adieu my Dear Father.

Your affectionate daughter
E. E. Hamtramck[203]

Folly must be Ellen Eliza's little sister, Florence, who would come to own our house with her younger sister, Eliza (Sarah Frances). Aunt Sally is the Selby daughter who would become John F. Hamtramck's third wife. Ellen Eliza expresses touching affection for the slaves, in particular, Celia. I wonder how reciprocal such sentiments were from the slaves.

Ellen Eliza seems like an agreeable girl judging from her letter, but barely two months later an unattractive message arrived at her father's in Shepherdstown. It is from Ellen Eliza's caretaker while she is away at school, Anne F. White, who complains:

Arcadia   June 22 1839
Dear Sir

It pains me exceedingly to be obliged to make any complaint of a child who must be so dear to her Father's heart, but feeling as sensibly as I do the responsibility I have assumed, duty and duty alone compels me to do so. During the past week Ellen has cast off my authority altogether, refusing to say her lessons or comply with the most simple request,

---

203 Hamtramck, Ellen Eliza, letter to John Francis Hamtramck, April 28, 1839. JFH Papers.

thus grieving me extremely. . . . Ellen can be, when she pleases, all that I could wish her, and her amiable and gentle deportment for. Those weeks previous to your visit proved to me that the will was all that was necessary. Her abilities are good if she will only apply herself—But I trust that the coming weeks will enable me to afford you as much of consolation, as I do now of pain.

With regard to the weekly report—I am sorry to be obliged to refuse what may have seemed a reasonable request, but I do not think it would be at all beneficial to Miss Taylor's children to send a report of this conduct to strangers. Their parents, while living, are in my opinion the only persons who should be made so intimately acquainted with these little faults which are in a great degree incident to childhood.

The trust you have reposed in me, dear Sir, is great, and I endeavor to be guided in my whole line of conduct towards your dear child by what, under Heaven seems to me that which will conduce most to her happiness and my own hopes of a reward in a world to come.

Begging you to remember me very affectionately to Miss Selby, believe me dear Sir with great respect yours most sincerely

Anne F. White

Ellen complained of this paper, and with reason as it is almost impossible to write on it.[204]

Not as bad as Mary to be sure, but wait a few moments—Anne White is not yet done with Ellen Eliza. First, however, the Miss Selby mentioned in Anne White's letter was Sally Selby who would become the third Mrs. Hamtramck. The previous letter from Ellen Eliza acknowledges her aunt Sally but not her mother, Eliza. As it happens, Eliza's death notice in the *Shepherdstown Register* gives her date of death as April 4, 1839, which may explain why she is absent from these two letters written soon after her death.[205]

The great mystery here, however, is why nobody says a word about Eliza Hamtramck in these letters. Was Ellen Eliza's misbehavior under Anne F. White's care a byproduct of her mother's death? And could Anne White not connect the mother's death with such behavior? Perhaps, but why not a single word of consolation about Eliza Hamtramck's death?

Within days of Anne White's letter, Ellen Eliza writes to her father and apologizes for having grieved him so much and promises to make up for

204 White, Anne F., letter to John Francis Hamtramck, June 22, 1839. JFH Papers.
205 *Martinsburg Gazette*, Martinsburg, Va., April 17, 1839, 2. BCIIS microfilm archives.

the faults of the previous two weeks. She goes on to chat about her goings and comings, the weather, meeting the acquaintances of Sister Mary, and not hearing from her grandma.[206] Much cheer but still no mention of her mother's recent death. Could it be that death occurred at such young ages in the early 1800's that people did not permit themselves to grieve the way we expect today? And were they constrained from mourning by prevailing social norms of the time? Although not entirely satisfying, I will leave these questions here.

Continuing with the discussion of Ellen Eliza's latest letter, the grandma she mentions would not be Mary's grandmother in Baltimore, nor of course, Walter Selby's deceased wife, Eleanor. The only one I can figure she could be is John Hamtramck's mother, who is identified as Rebecca McKenzie (1775–1851) in the family tree at the Historic Shepherdstown Museum noted in the previous chapter. In 1808, she married her second husband, Jesse Burgess Thomas (1777–1853), one of Illinois' first two Senators. He is best known as the author of the Missouri Compromise of 1820, which admitted Maine as a free state and Missouri as a slave state, thus maintaining a power balance between the North and the South in the United States Senate. After leaving politics in 1829, he moved to Mount Vernon, Ohio, where he lived the rest of his life.[207] In a few moments, we will learn that John F. Hamtramck visited Mount Vernon, Ohio, in 1837, doubtless to see his mother—the grandma Ellen Eliza mentions in her letter.

Three months later, Anne F. White weighs in again with another letter to John F. Hamtramck. She urges:

Dear Sir,   Arcadia Oct 10–/39

Understanding that you were to leave for St Louis on the 20—I again intrude myself upon you although my former letter remains unanswered. I write now to urge you again to make some arrangement for Ellen before you leave. Should you wish, at the close of the present six months, to place her with the Sisters in Frederick, whose school is at present quite small enough to admit her, you can do so without any trouble as it is so near us.

A letter from you to the Superior G. M. Agnes would I suppose be quite sufficient. They have seven competent and accomplished Sisters there, a

---

206 Hamtramck, Ellen Eliza, letter to John Francis Hamtramck, July 2, 1839. JFH Papers.
207 Wikipedia contributors, July 2, 2018, "Jesse B. Thomas." Retrieved from https://en.wikipedia.org/w/index.php?title=Jesse_B._Thomas&oldid=848558958

greater number than they have ever had before. The course of religious instruction pursued there is most excellent—the Revd. Mr. M. Ehoy prepares the children for their first communion.

Ellen cannot be benefitted by remaining here any longer and the change I propose will be for our mutual happiness. I am still of the opinion that a convent is the best place for her, all solicitous as I know you, a Catholic, to be for her religious principles.

No change need be made in her clothes. With wishes believe me dear Sir, with great respect

Anne F. White[208]

We hear no more about Ellen Eliza Hamtramck, Mary Rebecca Hamtramck, or any other family members in the JFH Papers after 1839. Ellen Eliza died in 1847. Her step-sister Mary Rebecca married, had two daughters, Mary and Julia, and died in 1852 according to the Hamtramck family tree noted earlier. Instead of family correspondence, military and business documents comprise the bulk of material in the JFH Papers after 1839.

Some noteworthy milestones in Colonel Hamtramck's life that I expected to find are missing from the JFH Papers. Never mentioned are his second wife Eliza's death in 1839 or his third marriage to Eliza's sister, Sally Selby, in 1842. Of course, no one expects these papers to be all-inclusive, even as voluminous as they are. They plainly only represent the remainders of all the documents and correspondence the family generated.

I will now return to some earlier letters, which I have held in reserve to keep the letters concerning Mary and Ellen Eliza Hamtramck together.

In 1837, Colonel Hamtramck's wife, Eliza, wrote to him from Shepherdstown while he was in Mount Vernon, Ohio, surely visiting his mother as noted a moment ago. He learns their infant daughter, Florence—future co-owner of our farmhouse with sister Eliza—took a violent cold, which monopolized all his wife's attention.

Eliza also mentions her husband's recent visit with the president in Washington and the warm reception he received but warns him that she fears his prospects are "not flattering." The president would either have been Andrew Jackson who left office on March 4, 1837, or Martin Van

208 White, Anne F., letter to letter to John Francis Hamtramck, October 10, 1839. JFH Papers.

103

Buren after that date. Hamtramck must have been applying for some office, but the letter does not disclose which one. Because of the intrigues of President Jackson or his circle to remove Hamtramck as Osage Indian agent in 1829 and the expiration of Jackson's term in office in 1837, I expect he had visited Van Buren.

Eliza writes enigmatically about selling Hannah. It is not clear who owns Hannah, but Eliza seems to need to get Hannah's consent for her own sale. A judge is the apparent prospective buyer, although it also could be Walter Selby. The purchase would not be permanent, but for a term of twenty years. Eliza believes Hannah will have no objection after she interviews her.

Eliza continues that daughter Ellen Eliza—before she went away to school in Frederick—practices the piano and Eliza believes she would make a first-rate pianist if she applied herself. Eliza mentions that her father, Walter Selby, has had chills, but that he is better again. She remarks that the weather has been charming and she has just enjoyed a long walk.[209]

Two weeks later Eliza writes another letter to her husband who was then in Cortland, New York. It holds troubling clues about the relationship between the Selby and Morgan families at that time. Eliza insists:

> Write fully immediately on the receipt of this.   April 27th 1837
> Dear Husband
>
> I have just had a conversation with Pa. He wishes you without fail to come on by the 15 of May if you can possibly arrange your business in New York your coming with thousands of dollars in your pocket. Lee has just been here. He says as certainly as the sun shines the sale made to Morgan and Hendricks be set aside for six weeks. Pa says if the land goes for one dollar he wishes it to go to the family meaning you.
>
> For God sake don't let Jacob Morgan buy the land. . . . As soon as Pa says this business is fixed he will make his will. He gives his property to Sally and me. The boys $250 apiece a year. I wish this they must not be beggars. . . . But oh God don't let the land go to strangers. . . . He is perfectly himself poor poor old man—no one to counsel and sustain him now. . . . I know your powers and if you succeed a mountain is removed from my heart and oh what exultation. Do help me heaven.
>
> If I had had the money I would have mounted the steps at Father's and give Jacob Morgan such a rebuke as never men had. . . . If I have written under

---

209 Hamtramck, Eliza C., letter to John Francis Hamtramck, April 14, 1837. JFH Papers.

excited feelings forgive me. Nature will be heard. It is my father who suffers. . . . Do what is best, but I think if Pa and you could meet, some arrangement might be made he says so the land goes in the family.

If it goes for one dollar he is satisfied. . . . Anything but Morgan. Consult your Pa. He is a man of excellent head. . . . All the children are well and happy. . . . Sally's love to the Judge and yourself. . . . I hope you are well and happy. Try and finish in New York before you come, but if possible be here by the 15th of May.

Your Devoted Wife, E. C. Hamtramck[210]

Walter Selby—"Pa" in the letter—must have to sell land, perhaps in connection with a notice of Commissioner's Sale issued March 15, 1837, which I will review in more detail shortly. The letter bespeaks a family feud between the Selby's and Jacob Morgan or the whole Morgan family. George Morgan, the first owner of our house, was a much older first cousin of Jacob's. Walter Selby had married George's sister, Eleanor, so the families had close ties. Jacob had recently built a mansion—Falling Spring—and was one of the wealthier citizens of Shepherdstown as was Walter Selby. Had one of the families offended the other? Had they crossed each other in business? I suspect the roots of this feud might have been a land deal gone wrong as an 1832 deed (No. 24) suggests.

Eliza makes her brothers sound unenterprising in her letter by wishing that they not become beggars. This judgement might have been a bit harsh. She does not name any particular brothers; however, at the time of this letter her brothers, Walter Jr.—who died two years later—and Henry, were still living, William was not, and I have no information on Thomas, John, and James. It appears that in later life Henry was able to provide a living for his household, at least in part from the income his farm produced.

During this period Colonel Hamtramck led several militias in Shepherdstown. One of them—the Potomac Rifle Company—resolved to invite surviving "war-worn" soldiers of the revolution from Frederick, Clarke, Berkeley, and Jefferson Counties to a military barbecue. The assembled group planned to march from Shepherdstown to the "festive ground," at Captain Lucas's grove on October 15, 1838.[211] Colonel

---

210 Hamtramck, Eliza C., letter to John Francis Hamtramck, April 27, 1837. JFH Papers.

211 *Martinsburg Gazette*, Martinsburg, Va., September 26, 1838, 3. BCHS microfilm archives.

Hamtramck commanded another local militia called the Shepherdstown Light Infantry. After Colonel Hamtramck's death, its members renamed it the Hamtramck Guard in his honor.[212] It fought for the Confederacy in the Civil War and few members escaped injury or death.[213]

Some years later, the Total Abstinence Society in Shepherdstown appointed Colonel Hamtramck to invite speakers, clergy, and the mayor to a mass meeting at the Presbyterian Church to celebrate George Washington's birthday after a parade on German Street. The society was hoping to use the event to revive "the great cause of Temperance," which had "been suffered to repose for a season—but for a season only."[214] It seems Hamtramck's services were in high demand due to his prestige.

War with Mexico

I found John F. Hamtramck's original 1846 commission as Colonel of the Virginia Regiment of Volunteers in the JFH Papers. Virginia Governor William Smith signed it. It cites Hamtramck's fidelity, courage, exemplary conduct, and the current war between the United States and the Republic of Mexico as the elements that inspired the commission.[215] The following celebratory article in the *Spirit of Jefferson* newspaper appeared after Colonel Hamtramck's commissioning:

> Wednesday [December 30, 1846]— was a day of universal interest and great parade in the city. It was understood that the Colonel of the first Regiment of Virginia Volunteers would arrive by the 12 o'clock train, and all the military turned out to receive him; and the whole population, of all sexes and ages, thronged the Capitol grounds to witness the pageant. The air was as balmy and the sun as bright as on a midsummer's day, and the scene was one of unusual splendor.
>
> The Colonel was escorted from the cars in the centre of the line, accompanied by Major Gwynn, Major Thompson of Jefferson,

---

212 *Shepherdstown Register*, Shepherdstown, W.Va., March 24, 1910, 1. LOC Chronicling America.

213 A Guide to Civil War Sites in Jefferson County, West Virginia, Society for Landmarks and Historic Homes, 1993. Retrieved from http://www.wvgeohistory.org /Portals/0/zoomify/URLDrivenPage2.htm?zImagePath=/Portals/0/zoomify/Civial _War_Markers_Map_-_Society_for_Landmarks_and_Historic_Homes_(C)_1993 _-_Back&zSkinPath=Assets/Skins/Default

214 *Martinsburg Gazette*, Martinsburg, Va., January 30, 1845, 2. BCHS microfilm archives.

215 Smith, William, governor of Virginia, commission of John F. Hamtramck as Colonel, December 22, 1846. JFH Papers.

Mr. Gallaher of the Senate, and Mr. Daniel of the Council. The procession, led by martial music, proceeded through the Capitol grounds to the mansion of the Governor, where the ceremony of introduction took place. As it passed along, the bosom of every soldier was cheered by the smiles of Richmond beauty, which thronged every window and place of observation; the heart of Col. Hamtramck beat high with emotion as he felt that every eye beamed brightly on him.

As the whole brilliant throng, with its stirring music, passed immediately by the windows of the Capitol, the members were all drawn out by the irresistible attraction, and did no business to-day. Col. Hamtramck is the greatest lion that has been in Richmond for many years, and his debut occasioned the most lively interest. Every body was anxious to get a look at him, and the ten thousand who assembled for this purpose were unanimous in the opinion that he was a splendid looking man. Every body seems gratified with the appointment, and his friends, are delighted. He said himself, that this was the proudest day of his life. May he receive such a welcome on his return from Mexico![216]

The next year Colonel Hamtramck wrote a two-verse poem at the Buena Vista headquarters about an idealized soldier missing his family and far from home. Although probably not great poetry, it marks a man of broader interests and abilities than his government and military posts might ordinarily have stirred. The second verse intones:

His thoughts were on his distant home,
The wife, who missed him there,
The children, whose weak, falt'ring steps,
Needed his tender care,
And tears were seen to gather
In the stern soldier's eye –
But quick he turned at Duty's call
And hush'd was every sigh.[217]

The header at the top of the primary source for the poem declares that it was "Written by J. F. Hamtramck in Mexico 1846." I checked the handwriting in Hamtramck's business ledgers, and it matches the script of the poem but not the header. I believe someone added the header later but that the date should have been 1847. Colonel Hamtramck did not leave for Mexico until that year as confirmed by the date of a send-off dinner—January 29, 1847—held in his honor at the Entler Hotel. The Historic

---

216 Virginia Legislature, "Correspondence of the *Spirit of Jefferson*, Richmond, Monday, December 28, 1846," *Spirit of Jefferson*, January 8, 1847, 2. Retrieved from http://www .wvgeohistory.org/Portals/0/newspapers/Spirit%20of%20Jefferson%201847_01_8.PDF
217 Hamtramck, John. F., poem, 1847. JFH Papers.

Shepherdstown Museum possesses an invitation to this dinner written in Walter Selby's aging handwriting, which is identifiable when compared with his 1795–1796 ledger handwriting although it is much less flowing.

An 1847 news article describes how Colonel Hamtramck's Regiment of Virginia Volunteers celebrated American Independence Day "on the soil of their enemy, and the theatre of one of the most brilliant victories of the war," near Buena Vista, Mexico. General Wool, Colonel Hamtramck, and their staff reviewed some 3,000 American troops followed by a dinner at a public-house in Saltillo, Mexico. An officer read the Declaration of Independence, and the regimental band played "Hail Columbia." Dinner consisted of roast pigs, ham, cabbage, lamb, turkeys, geese, a variety of vegetables, rice pudding, hot cake, and fruit.

After dinner, the tablecloth came off, and Colonel Hamtramck took charge as president of the affair. Attendees drank toasts interspersed with patriotic songs by the regiment's glee club. Among the twenty-four toasts offered, Colonel Hamtramck's was to General Wool, "the hero of Buena Vista and Plattsburg." In the end, the party adjourned to camp including "a few a little elevated by the exhilarating effects of the wine." The writer of the article claimed to belong to the Total Temperance Society, and therefore could not attest to the qualities of the wine.[218]

Another artifact in the JFH Papers is a record of Colonel Hamtramck's military orders issued in November and December 1847, at the Buena Vista Headquarters. Some of the orders grant leave for ill soldiers, one commands an arrest, and one directs a captain of one regiment to deliver six pack mules and saddles to the captain of another regiment.[219] After the war ended, Colonel Hamtramck became military governor of the State of Saltillo, Mexico, for several months in 1848 before returning home.[220]

Return to Shepherdstown from Mexico

Back in Shepherdstown after the War with Mexico, Colonel Hamtramck occupied himself with public concerns. The Valley Agricultural Society

218 *Spirit of Jefferson*, Charles Town, Va., August 13, 1847, 3. LOC Chronicling America.
219 Hamtramck, John. F., military orders, November 25, 1847 to December 8, 1847. JFH Papers.
220 Hamtramck, John Francis, "Virtual American Biographies," 2000. Retrieved from http://www.famousamericans.net/johnfrancishamtramck/

named him a marshal for its Agricultural and Horticultural Exhibition near Charles Town in October 1852. He oversaw judging for the best bushels of corn, wheat, oats, rye, timothy-grass seed, clover seed, and Irish potatoes.[221]

The governor appointed him to administer a local election of Electoral College representatives for the presidential election the same year.[222] Colonel Hamtramck also served as a magistrate of the court in Jefferson County.[223] Following in his father-in-law's footsteps, John F. Hamtramck was mayor of Shepherdstown from 1850 to 1854.

People remembered his wit long after his death. A writer related the following anecdote in 1911 to illustrate :

> He [Colonel Hamtramck] had brought with him from the Mexican campaign a young black mustang colt, a fine rider, though at times exhibiting the qualities of the broncho. Though he was a Catholic, he kindly loaned this pony to a Methodist preacher to go out to some country chapel, and surely not with any malicious intent. Methodist preachers from their itinerant experience are generally good jockeys, but a short distance from town the pony pitched off the preacher, who went overhead, sprawling upon the roadway. The Colonel remarked that his Protestant brethren should surely give him due credit for his help in 'spreading the gospel.'[224]

The final page of John F. Hamtramck's life was written on April 21, 1858, the date of his death. He died at his home after an illness of less than a week of diseases of the kidneys, liver, and spine. His obituary described him as a kind husband, doting father, and faithful friend. It told that "Col. Hamtramck was emphatically a military man," who had devoted his life to "the profession of arms. . . . He met the last great enemy as might have been expected of a brave man, with calmness and composure."[225]

An invaluable description of Colonel Hamtramck's life and style appeared in 1884. H. Hunt wrote it in the same article that he wrote about three of

---

221 *Spirit of Jefferson*, Charles Town, Va., October 12, 1852, 3. LOC Chronicling America.

222 *Spirit of Jefferson*, Charles Town, Va., October 12, 1852, 3. LOC Chronicling America.

223 *Shepherdstown Register*, Shepherdstown, W. Va., September 28, 1911, 1. LOC Chronicling America.

224 *Shepherdstown Register*, Shepherdstown, W. Va., September 28, 1911, 1. LOC Chronicling America.

225 *Shepherdstown Register*, Shepherdstown, W. Va., April 24, 1858, 2. LOC Chronicling America.

the Selby boys in the *Shepherdstown Register*, as pointed out under Walter Selby's entry in the previous chapter. Hunt reminisced about many of the townspeople of that time including Hamtramck, whom he described as large and strictly military. He wrote that President Adams appointed Hamtramck as Indian agent and President Jackson removed him. He describes Hamtramck as down on Jackson because he removed him from a "fat office." I do not believe his removal is quite so clear-cut, based on some documents among the JFH Papers already discussed in this chapter, which contradict it. Hunt describes Hamtramck's mode of travel thus:

> An old-style carriage with four horses and a very important darky dressed in the height of fashion. . . . Behind there was another darky standing up, holding the straps, a footman.

When his carriage arrived, everyone came out as if it was a circus parade. The writer supposed that Hamtramck had long since died, or he would have heard of him in the Civil War.[226] He was correct on that point.

Financial Trouble

The following material derives mostly from sources other than the JFH Papers. But it did not make sense to break it up and spread it among separate sections of the text. Since it all relates to some of Walter Selby's unmistakable financial problems, and some of it comes from the JFH Papers, I have permitted this connection to govern the placement of all the material here.

We get an inkling of financial impropriety from an 1826 letter to Walter Selby in the JFH Papers from someone in Baltimore. The message is about an unpaid promissory note, but the signature is undecipherable. The writer asserts:

> Dear Sir   Baltimore June 27th, 1826

> We wrote you on Feb. 21st last in reply to yours of the 19th, and proposed your paying half the amount of your note in all May and the balance in Oct. and not having heard from you, and the period of payment of the first mostly being now a month over due, we are rather surprised.

> Thus always with great reluctance, we resort to coercive measures, but

---

226 *Shepherdstown Register*, Shepherdstown, W.Va., January 26, 1884, 3. LOC Chronicling America.

when a proposition so reasonable as the above is not acceded to, we have reason to conclude that payment is not to be expected. . . . [W]e shall wait however one month from this time.

Your obdt [illegible]
[illegible][227]

Eleven years later, Walter Selby shows up uncomfortably in the public record. By this time he was in business with son-in-law John F. Hamtramck. Disturbingly, the following decree for hundreds of acres of Walter Selby's lands—doubtless connected to Eliza Hamtramck's April 27, 1837 letter—appeared in the *Martinsburg Gazette* in March 1837:

COMMISSIONER'S SALE

In pursuance of a decree of the Circuit Superior Court of Law and Chancery for the County of Frederick [Virginia], rendered on the 24th of October 1836, in the case of Peter Hoover's executors against Walter B. Selby, etc., will be offered for sale, at public auction.

On the 26th day of April next, at Daniel Entler's Tavern, in Shepherdstown, the following Tracts or Parcels of Land belonging to the said Walter B. Selby, lying adjoining each other in the County of Jefferson, about 3 miles from Shepherdstown—viz:

[A] tract of 85 Acres conveyed to said Selby by Rawleigh Morgan [Colonel William Morgan's son] and Lydia his wife, by deed bearing date April 28th, 1800 [Deed No. 2].

[A] tract containing 5 ½ acres conveyed to the same by the same, by deed, bearing date December 22, 1802 [Deed No. 3].

A tract containing 9 acres, 1 rood, and 10 poles, conveyed to same by Peter Hoover, by deed dated January 14th, 1811 [Deed No. 7].

An Undivided third part of a tract of 200 Acres, conveyed to same, by Rawleigh Morgan, Jr., by deed dated October 25th, 1811 [Deed No. 8].

A tract containing 50 Acres being the fourth part of a larger tract containing 200 Acres, which fourth part was conveyed to the same by William Morgan, Jr., by deed dated January 8, 1813 [Deed No. 10]; . . .

[A] tract containing 50 Acres, being the fourth part of a larger tract of 200 Acres, which said tract of 50 Acres, was conveyed to same by Simon Morgan by deed dated February 4th, 1814 [Deed No. 12]. . . . So much or so many of the said tracts of land will be sold as may be necessary to raise the sum of $3,076.96, with the interest of $1,761.65, a part thereof, from December the 8th, 1830 until the day of sale, and all costs

227 Letter to Walter B. Selby, June 27, 1826. JFH Papers.

attending said sale. The lands are deemed inferior to none in the country in quality and location.

JOHN H. McENDREE, Commissioner   March 15, 1837-ts[228]

The same John McEndree rented the deceased Walter Selby's storehouse twenty years later as noted in the previous chapter. This point suggests that McEndree was a merchant at that time.

Without examining the corresponding court records, we do not know the reason Peter Hoover's estate made this claim against Walter Selby. Could it have been a dispute over payment for land purchases or unpaid business debts? Peter Hoover granted Deeds No. 7 and No. 13 to Walter Selby over twenty-one years before this court decree. Furthermore, Peter Hoover must have died before 1815, as proven by Deed No. 13. The 200-acre tract partially granted in Deed No. 8 and mentioned in this decree is the property where our log farmhouse stands. Another unknown is why the Court in Frederick County, Virginia, issued this decree when all the land in question was in Jefferson County, Virginia.

Yet another ruling appeared in the *Martinsburg Gazette* in 1838, entitled "Public Sale of Valuable Jefferson Land," with the same details as the 1837 decree. It named Peter Hoover's executors as Jacob Hess and William Taylor. It does not mention the amount necessary to pay the claim or the interest on it. Special Commissioner Henry Berry signed it on March 14, 1838, at Shepherdstown.[229] I did not find any sources that could explain why this mandate turned up a year after the first, or so long after Peter Hoover's death.

On the exact same day as the 1838 decree, John F. Hamtramck placed an offer for sale of Walter Selby's Scrabble Farm northeast of Shepherdstown for $3,500.[230] The sale of Walter Selby's lands named in the two court decrees and his Scrabble Farm never happened. As far as I can determine, all of these parcels were still intact and under Selby's ownership according to the 1852 tax map.

---

228 "Commissioner's Sale," *Martinsburg Gazette*, Martinsburg, Va., March 15, 1837. BCHS microfilm archives.

229 "Public Sale of Valuable Jefferson Land," *Martinsburg Gazette*, Martinsburg, Va., March 14, 1838. BCHS microfilm archives.

230 *Martinsburg Gazette*, Martinsburg, Va., March 14, 1838, 2. BCHS microfilm archives.

Suspecting the details of this case might reveal some compelling circumstances of Walter Selby's life, I called the Frederick County, Virginia, court clerk who stated that their casebooks only go back to the 1870's. The earlier books might have perished in the Civil War.

On May 16, 1837, Eliza wrote to her husband, still in Mount Vernon, Ohio, about her father, Walter Selby, selling land of which she maintained that "there is no better property."[231] This followed her April 27 letter imploring her husband to return home to prevent a land sale to Jacob Morgan. These letters clearly relate to the 1837 Commissioner's Sale, but exactly how is unclear. Four months later, Walter Selby drafted a never-executed instrument appointing attorneys, including John F. Hamtramck, to sell a 198-acre tract he bought from Peter Hoover's executors. This land corresponds to Deed No. 13 of June 8, 1815, but is not one of the tracts listed in the 1837 or 1838 decrees of public sale. The instrument declares that Walter Selby is selling to satisfy his debt to Peter Hoover's executors. It sounds to me like he might have been hoping to sell this tract instead of those in the public decrees. Although he paid seventy dollars per acre in 1815 for the 198-acre tract, he was willing to sell for fifty dollars per acre in 1837.[232] I found no record that this sale ever occurred.

Another clue I have about Walter Selby's possible financial troubles is a court judgment dated May 16, 1839. The Jefferson County Circuit Superior Court of Law and Chancery ordered Walter Selby and John F. Hamtramck to pay a penalty of $550 and deliver certain property mentioned in an obligation they executed on January 24, and failed to provide.[233] This judgment does not appear to be related to the 1837 and 1838 decrees of public sale because it originates from Jefferson and not Frederick County.

Through an 1837 deed—not included in Appendix A—Walter Selby gives the residue of his household furniture to his youngest daughter, Sally, due to the love and affection he feels for her. He also disclosed in the deed that some years earlier he gave, by way of advancement, sundry articles of furniture and other movable property to his eldest daughter, Eliza, intending the residue to go to Sally. There were forty-seven items listed

---

231 Hamtramck, Eliza C., letter to John Francis Hamtramck, May 16, 1837. JFH Papers.

232 Selby, Walter B., legal instrument, September 1837. JFH Papers.

233 Crawford, Mr. Jr., court judgment, May 16, 1839. JFH Papers.

in the annex to this deed, including bedsteads, bureaus, tables, carpets, china, a family Bible, a sleigh, a cow, and a horse.[234]

Why Walter Selby granted these things to his daughter, Sally, long before he died and while still living in the Wynkoop Tavern I cannot answer without further research. Could it have been that he was trying to shield his belongings from public sale because of the 1837 court decree against him? The financial Panic of 1837 might have precipitated Walter Selby's evident contemporaneous financial troubles and premature disposal of personal property.

Surprisingly, Walter Selby's 1837 deed mentions furniture he had given to daughter, Eliza, years before—presumably the furniture she hotly demanded in her 1826 letter from St. Louis. Did Eliza ever actually get her furniture? I think she finally did by the time she and Colonel Hamtramck moved back to Shepherdstown from St. Louis.

The last indication of some financial difficulty in Walter Selby's life came in 1847. Recall as noted in Chapter 2 that he and others petitioned the town council not to levy any taxes on the citizens that year. Although he was land rich, he may have been cash poor by then—a situation likely related to his age and reduced or no income from his once thriving business.

In the next chapter, we will find out who the occupants of our farmhouse were for much of the nineteenth century and beyond. We will get some fleeting glimpses of their lives at the farm and while some of their stories are amusing, others are horrifying. Read on.

---

234 Pendleton, 15.

CHAPTER 7 TENANT FARM MANAGERS

THROUGHOUT MOST OF my research, I was unable to find any information on the tenants who lived at our farmhouse during its long period of absentee ownership lasting roughly a hundred and thirty years through 1946. That changed once I discovered the Library of Congress's Chronicling America project, which allowed me to search the names of the farm's owners online in the *Spirit of Jefferson* and *Shepherdstown Register* newspapers. This type of search enabled me to associate a farmhouse tenant name with nearly every decade of absentee ownership. The information these searches yielded changed my thinking about what kind of tenants would have wanted to rent or live in the Selby farmhouse.

The tenants' names and news stories about them follow. The date ranges after their names are the best approximations I can infer of their years of farmhouse occupancy.

John Sigler 1818–1860

The earliest tenant of our farmhouse I know of was John Sigler. His name appeared in an interesting item in the *Shepherdstown Register*. In 1857, an Overseers of the Poor report listed a twelve-dollar payment to him for boarding Samuel Show for six months.[235] Samuel Show may have been ill when John Sigler took him in as he died at age 65 in June of 1857.[236]

This news conveys that John Sigler was not among the poor himself and that Jefferson County considered him an honorable citizen fit to receive public funds for charitable work. It also foreshadows a possible connection with the next known tenant of the farm, George Show. Perhaps there was an ongoing association between the farm owner, Henry Selby, and the Shows. We know George Show was much younger than Samuel signaling that he might have been Samuel's son.

John Sigler died in 1860. His executors advertised his large estate for sale southeast of Shepherdstown at the Selby farm. This ad is how I first identified him as a tenant at the farm. He had farmed the place for forty-two

---

235 *Shepherdstown Register*, Shepherdstown, Va., August 1, 1857, 3. LOC Chronicling America.

236 *Shepherdstown Register*, Shepherdstown, Va., July 4, 1857, 2. LOC Chronicling America.

years before the Civil War.[237] His tenure coincided with Walter Selby's and the first few years of Henry Selby's ownership of the farm.

His estate sale included horses, cattle, hogs, sheep, large quantities of grain—wheat, rye, and oats—plows, wagons, household furnishings, and a ten-plate stove.[238] I have seen such a ten-plate stove in the kitchen of the General Adam Stephen house in Martinsburg. Its plates are really doors on all four sides of a rectangular cast-iron box on legs. It included an oven and a fixed top for surface cooking. It could also be used for heating of course.

John Sigler owned substantial personal property and even received public funds for taking in the poor. His appearance in my research shifted my thinking about the status of our farmhouse tenants. Instead of renting their farm to families in near poverty the Selby family might have employed experienced farmers to oversee its operation. Living at the house might have been like a fringe benefit, although there may have been a fee charged for it. This is not the image of the country types Latrobe described in his journal.

Consider the ample 1840's south addition, including the updating of the entire farmhouse with chic Greek Revival wood trim throughout, and the spacious 1929 west addition. They speak of the farm owners' desires over time to attract, keep, and accommodate the growing families of competent managers rather than to cater to indigent farmers with few choices.

Since John Sigler died in 1860 and the local press went dark during the Civil War, we may never know who the tenants were or anything about what they experienced during that turbulent time. Upon resuming publication after the war, the *Shepherdstown Register* reported that John's wife, Sarah, had died on September 10, 1862—only days before the Battle of Antietam—at age 68. She might have lived on at the farm with some of her offspring after her husband's death, and one or more of them might have stayed on after her death. Hence, some of Sarah's children might have received soldiers from the Battle of Antietam at the farmhouse. Indeed, I believe this is likely considering Mary Bedinger Mitchell's account of

---

237 *Shepherdstown Register*, Shepherdstown, W. Va., September 2, 1909, 3. LOC Chronicling America.

238 *Shepherdstown Register*, Shepherdstown, Va., July 21, 1860, 2. LOC Chronicling America.

the wounded and dying from that battle overflowing into the farmhouses around Shepherdstown.

John Sigler's son and lifelong resident of the Shepherdstown area, Robert Michael Douglas Sigler, died in 1909 at seventy-seven years of age. He was born at the Selby farmhouse in 1832 and "was quiet, undemonstrative in his manner, but kind-hearted and upright in all his ways. He was never married. . . . "[239]

George Show (?)–1873

The next time we learn of a tenant at the farm was when he was leaving it. Having decided to quit farming in 1873, George Show advertised for sale at auction all his livestock and farming tools. The auction was to take place at his residence on Henry Selby's farm a mile and a half south of Shepherdstown.[240] This is our farmhouse and George Show was living there and farming the land. This ad is the only record I have of when he lived at the farm.

In 1866, the Shepherdstown Register reported George Show was surveyor of the roads from Shepherdstown to Harper's Ferry, implying he had not yet taken employment at the Selby farm.[241] In 1867, he bought a house at auction for $1,780 on the corner opposite the Entler Hotel.[242] Thus, it looks like he lived at the farm for less than six years.

George Show is named as one of the defendants in a complicated court case brought by James Orendorf in 1869. The case had to do with who owed what to whom for James Orendorf's deceased father William's hiring out of a Negro boy named Warner.[243] The court notice does not specify whether Warner's hiring took place before or after the end of slavery or what George Show's role might have been.

---

239 *Shepherdstown Register*, Shepherdstown, W. Va., September 2, 1909, 3. LOC Chronicling America.

240 *Shepherdstown Register*, Shepherdstown, W. Va., April 4, 1873, 3. LOC Chronicling America.

241 *Shepherdstown Register*, Shepherdstown, W. Va., January 20, 1866, 2. LOC Chronicling America.

242 *Shepherdstown Register*, Shepherdstown, W. Va., October 12, 1867, 2. LOC Chronicling America.

243 *Shepherdstown Register*, Shepherdstown, W. Va., October 9, 1869, 3. LOC Chronicling America.

That same year, George's wife worked on a committee to raise funds for instruments for a town band at a ladies' fair during the Christmas holidays. The committee planned to collect money by "soliciting contributions and preparing articles of different kinds to be exposed for sale at the Fair."[244]

George Show's 1873 advertisement listed workhorses, mares, cattle, milking cows, many hogs and piglets, wagons, plows, harrows, a buggy, and wheat and corn implements. He mentions that there is also about eighty acres of wheat in the ground. This gives us a good idea of the types of livestock and some of the crops the farm produced in the 1870's.[245]

The *familysearch.com* website reveals that George Show was born in 1817 or 1818. His wife's name was Margaret E., and they had four children at home—Ann, Ellen, Daniel, and Ada—according to the 1870 U.S. Census. I chose this census year because it is the closest to the 1873 date of the Shows' departure from the farmhouse.

I cannot determine from the limited information in the 1870 census whether the Shows were already living at our house at that time. In 1873, the family of six would have been living in the original log core of the house with its 1840's addition. George Show would have been about fifty-five years old.

A few months before leaving the Selby farm, he bought about eleven acres of land east of Shepherdstown. This parcel would not have been large enough for a farming livelihood even if he had kept his livestock and farm equipment. He might have turned to a different line of work at that point.

George Show died in 1892. He belonged to the Reformed Church and was "a man of many excellent traits of character," according to his obituary.[246] His widow and other family members sold his acreage to other Show family members in 1895, although the deed was not recorded until

---

244 *Shepherdstown Register*, Shepherdstown, W.Va., November 13, 1869, 2. LOC Chronicling America.
245 *Shepherdstown Register*, Shepherdstown, W.Va., April 4, 1873, 3. LOC Chronicling America.
246 *Shepherdstown Register*, Shepherdstown, W.Va., November 18, 1892, 3. LOC Chronicling America.

1918.[247] The 1900 U.S. Census lists Margaret Show, then aged seventy-eight, living with children and grandchildren outside Shepherdstown, but gives no precise location. It also records that she had a total of eleven children during her lifetime, but only five were living. She died in 1901.[248]

Robert Cookus 1873 (?)–1878

The next known tenant at the farmhouse was Robert Cookus who might have moved in soon after George Show moved out. The Cookus family dates back to the earliest days of Shepherdstown history. Robert Cookus must be a descendant.

The *Shepherdstown Register* published an advertisement in 1878 by Robert Cookus who said he was leaving the state and was to sell all his personal property at auction at the Selby farm where he lived. He was moving to Rockingham County, Virginia. In another article of the same date, the newspaper described him as one of the best farmers and an honest citizen whose departure the community regretted.[249]

His property included many of the types of items George Show sold at his auction in 1873 plus things like bedsteads, bedding, bureaus, tables, chairs, carpets, stoves—including a No. 1 cooking stove—and "three stands of bees."[250] He might have bought his livestock and farm equipment at George Show's 1873 auction. His ad also suggests that stoves—most likely for burning wood or coal—heated the house at that time. The fireplace flues might have provided outlets for some of the stovepipes. Wood or coal stoves might also have heated the south addition, but any traces of their stovepipe openings through the walls are gone. We have found lumps of coal in the soil around the farmhouse—possible remnants of stove fuel.

The *Shepherdstown Register* reported that someone killed and cleaned a superb lamb at Henry Selby's farm in 1876. It stated that the lamb belonged to Robert Cookus who lived on the farm. Of course, no one ever

---

247 Jefferson County Clerk, *Deed Book 116*, Page 414, August 28, 1918.

248 *Shepherdstown Register*, Shepherdstown, W.Va., September 12, 1901, 3. LOC Chronicling America.

249 *Shepherdstown Register*, Shepherdstown, W.Va., March 9, 1878, 2. LOC Chronicling America.

250 *Shepherdstown Register*, Shepherdstown, W.Va., February 2, 1878, 2. LOC Chronicling America.

found the perpetrator.[251] Here is another species of livestock raised on the farm. The only other news we have of Robert Cookus is that he lost some chickens, hens, and eggs to a thief in 1877.[252]

A news article appears about this time that leads me to believe Henry Selby was always actively involved in the workings of his farm. Recall that the *Shepherdstown Register* reported that Henry Selby's wheat crop was the best of the season in 1878, as mentioned in Chapter 5.[253] I believe it is noteworthy that the article attributed the wheat crop to Henry Selby rather than to the tenant who produced it. The tenant responsible for the 1878 wheat crop would not have been Robert Cookus who left the farm before the 1878 growing season had begun.

I did not find the names of any other tenants between Robert Cookus and the next known tenant, William W. Myers. Since the time between these tenants possibly spanned more than the entire decade of the 1880's, there may have been more than one tenant during the period.

William W. Myers 1890 (?)–1897

The earliest article I found placing William Myers at our farm was written in 1890. It recounted how, while working on a fence row, he stepped on a nail, which ran clear through his foot. The article told that the wound was extremely painful, but that Myers was able to get around a little two weeks later.[254]

William Myers's bad luck kept surfacing. In 1891, the Shepherdstown Register reported that someone left a gate open and his cattle strayed into town. They got on the railroad tracks and collided with a locomotive, which "as usual, came out best." The resultant bellowing broke the night's sleep of the neighborhood. About the same time, someone set fire to a

251 *Shepherdstown Register*, Shepherdstown, W. Va., August 19, 1876, 2. LOC Chronicling America.

252 *Shepherdstown Register*, Shepherdstown, W. Va., May 12, 1877, 2. LOC Chronicling America.

253 *Shepherdstown Register*, Shepherdstown, W. Va., August 24, 1878, 2. LOC Chronicling America.

254 *Shepherdstown Register*, Shepherdstown, W. Va., September 19, 1890, 3. LOC Chronicling America.

stack of straw in William Myers's field. About a week later some dogs killed three of his hogs.[255]

A humorous article citing William Myers, titled "Swapped a Horse for a Few Chickens," appears in the Shepherdstown Register in 1894 and reads:

> About two o'clock last Saturday morning George Demory, who lives with Wm. W. Myers on the Selby farm, about two miles from town, heard the chickens squawking very suspiciously. He went out to investigate, taking for company David Freeman and Mr. Myers's uncle who was there on a visit. Near the barn they came upon a man with both hands full of chickens. They at once opened fire upon him, and he started off on a run, with all three in full pursuit.
>
> He made such good time, however, that he soon disappeared in the darkness. Returning to the barn, Mr. Demory and his friends found standing quietly near the barn a fine, big bay mare, saddled and bridled, and some strings to be probably used for tying the chickens. The owner of the horse has not yet returned for it. He is probably in some place kicking himself for the bad trade he made, unless the horse was stolen too.[256]

An 1896 report confirmed that William Myers still lived at the farm and his wife's name was Jennie.[257] The following year this sad article appeared:

> An elderly colored man was working for William Myers on the Selby farm. He fell on the way to his nearby home, was picked up and carried there, only to die a few minutes later.[258]

This episode reinforces the theory that residents of our farmhouse were hired managers who oversaw laborers. The unfortunate elderly laborer might have lived in the collapsed wood-frame house directly across Engle Molers Road from our farmhouse property. In 1897, William Myers sent the *Shepherdstown Register* a curious egg from the Selby farm, which had a handle on one end. The article stated that "[t]he convenience of this sort

---

255 *Shepherdstown Register*, Shepherdstown, W.Va., September 11, 1891, 3. LOC Chronicling America.

256 *Shepherdstown Register*, Shepherdstown, W.Va., June 28, 1894, 3. LOC Chronicling America.

257 *Shepherdstown Register*, Shepherdstown, W.Va., May 14, 1896, 3. LOC Chronicling America.

258 *Shepherdstown Register*, Shepherdstown, W.Va., December 2, 1897, 3. LOC Chronicling America.

of hen fruit can readily be seen."[259] I found another article reporting that William Myers had received a visitor at the Wysong farm in 1897.[260] This item confirms that he had left the Selby farm that year to work at a farm a little further east along Engle Molers Road. In 1899, the *Shepherdstown Register* reported that "Mr. William Myers, the hustling farmer who runs the Wysong place, cut 47 ½ acres of wheat in one day."[261] This is the last time we hear of him.

Charles F. Byers 1905 (?)–1920

Another tenant farm manager's name surfaced in a 1905 advertisement. In the ad, Charles F. Byers offered to sell personal property and prize-winning registered stock "worthy of breeders' attention," at the Selby farm.[262] He had won multiple prizes for his livestock at various agricultural fairs in the mid-Atlantic states over many years before this ad appeared.

The 1909 article already cited about tenant John Sigler's son's death mentions Byers as the current tenant at the Selby farm.[263] But by January of 1910, Charles Byers had become a dealer of Studebaker wagons, buggies, and surreys alongside all manner of farm equipment in Shepherdstown.[264] This is an unusual career move after spending years breeding, exhibiting, and selling prize-winning livestock. In 1911, Byers even took out a large illustrated ad on the front page of the *Shepherdstown Register* praising the craftsmanship of Studebaker wagons.[265] The same firm that manufactured these wagons and also made Studebaker automobiles.

---

259 *Shepherdstown Register*, Shepherdstown, W. Va., May 27, 1897, 3. LOC Chronicling America.

260 *Shepherdstown Register*, Shepherdstown, W. Va., October 28, 1897, 3. LOC Chronicling America.

261 *Shepherdstown Register*, Shepherdstown, W. Va., June 29, 1899, 3. LOC Chronicling America.

262 *Shepherdstown Register*, Shepherdstown, W. Va., October 26, 1905, 3. LOC Chronicling America.

263 *Shepherdstown Register*, Shepherdstown, W. Va., September 2, 1909, 3. LOC Chronicling America.

264 *Shepherdstown Register*, Shepherdstown, W. Va., April 7, 1910, 2. LOC Chronicling America.

265 *Shepherdstown Register*, Shepherdstown, W. Va., September 28, 1911, 1. LOC Chronicling America.

While still at our house on the Selby farm in November 1910, Charles F. Byers advertised livestock and farm implements "at his home one and a half miles south of town on the road leading to Bakerton," and stated his intention to discontinue farming.[266] The location he gives for his home is undoubtedly that of our farmhouse. The road to Bakerton today would be Engle Molers Road where our farmhouse is situated and not Shepherdstown Pike where the Red Pump farmhouse—also on the Selby farm property—was located.

The reason to mention the Red Pump farm here is that there may be confusion about which farmhouse Charles Byers lived in. Sisters Florence Shepherd and Eliza Williamson jointly owned the property that encompassed the Red Pump farmhouse and our farmhouse (Wheatland) until 1914. In March 1913, a *Shepherdstown Register* article placed Charles Byers as the tenant at Florence Shepherd's farm, at which time he was moving to a house on Princess Street in town to be close to his Studebaker outlet. The article noted that he had left his son, William, to run Mrs. Shepherd's farm.[267]

Apparently, the Red Pump farm had become associated with Mrs. Shepherd long before the 1914 division of property delivered it exclusively to her. Another article in December 1913 tells of a straw stack overturning in a gale at Mrs. Shepherd's Red Pump farm then tenanted by Harry Byers and Fred Cook.[268] Harry Byers must have been a relative of Charles Byers, but plainly not his son, William. If, as noted in the previous paragraph, William Byers had taken charge of the Red Pump farm upon his father's leaving it, only eight or so months later a different Byers (Harry) already occupied it. Although not impossible, I do not believe it likely that William Byers had taken over operations at the Red Pump farm only to leave it a short time later. I think the writer of the March 1913 article mistakenly placed Charles Byers at the Red Pump farm instead of Harry Byers—an error the author of the December 1913 article appears to have corrected.

---

266 *Shepherdstown Register*, Shepherdstown, W. Va., November 24, 1910, 3. LOC Chronicling America.

267 *Shepherdstown Register*, Shepherdstown, W. Va., March 27, 1913, 3. LOC Chronicling America.

268 *Shepherdstown Register*, Shepherdstown, W. Va., December 11, 1913, 3. LOC Chronicling America.

By chance, another article on the same page as the previously noted March 1913 article implicitly places William Byers—and by extrapolation his father Charles—at our farmhouse. The article tells the tragic tale of a fourteen-year-old schoolboy named Griggs Flanagan. Griggs's mother was driving him home to Bakerton from school in town when their light wagon collided with a heavy farm wagon drawn by four horses, which had taken fright. The poor boy was run over and died almost instantly, while his mother survived without serious injury. The accident occurred as mother and son descended the hill on Engle Molers Road between Shepherdstown Pike and our farmhouse. Within a few moments, William Byers, who was at work in a field along the road, was on the scene. This report is a convincing association of William Byers and his father, Charles, with our farmhouse situated as it is along Engle Molers Road.

It appears Charles Byers had switched back to agriculture from wagon sales by 1919 when he bought ninety-three lambs from W. A. Fulk.[269] There is no record of what he did with the lambs. Late that year Byers placed an ad for ten or twelve thousand feet of oak boards, cordwood, and other lumber, which he was selling at Eliza Williamson's farm where he told buyers they could find him most of the time.[270] He ran similar ads through 1920. By 1919, Eliza Williamson was the sole owner of our farmhouse. I suspect that William Byers might have stayed on at our farmhouse after 1913 and been there when his parents returned by 1919. I will also present another reason I believe Charles Byers lived at our farmhouse through 1920, rather than at the Red Pump farmhouse, under the Skinner family entry, which follows shortly.

Charles Byers sold his business property on Princess Street for $4,250 in 1921.[271] In 1922 he and his wife were living in Berkeley County and reported to be entertaining guests there.[272] This is the last time Charles F. Byers appeared in the local newspapers. Harry Byers was still living at

---

269 *Shepherdstown Register*, Shepherdstown, W.Va., June 26, 1919, 3. LOC Chronicling America.

270 *Shepherdstown Register*, Shepherdstown, W.Va., December 18, 1919, 3. LOC Chronicling America.

271 *Shepherdstown Register*, Shepherdstown, W.Va., October 27, 1921, 5. LOC Chronicling America.

272 *Shepherdstown Register*, Shepherdstown, W.Va., July 13, 1922, 5. LOC Chronicling America.

the Red Pump farmhouse in 1922 according to an article that noted his subscription renewal to the *Shepherdstown Register.*[273] By 2011, when we bought the Selby farmhouse, the Red Pump farmhouse was lying in a heap of rubble by the side of Shepherdstown Pike. For continuity, I have called our farm the Selby farm long after its last Selby owner (Henry) died in 1898. However, the George Morgan farm is the name I prefer.

Howard T. and Mary L. Skinner 1920–1946

I will now introduce the last tenants who occupied our farmhouse. The 1920 U.S. Census lists Howard Skinner as head of his household at age thirty-two with wife, Mary, and four children. The census lists him as a farmer who rented his farm. His census entry is the first one on Route 31, known as Engle Molers Road. In 1920, there were no other dwellings along the south side of Engle Molers Road between our farmhouse and Shepherdstown Pike. The census lists John Wysong as a near neighbor whose family was located a little further east on Engle Molers Road according to the 1852 tax map. Therefore, we can be quite confident that Howard T. Skinner lived in our particular farmhouse in 1920.[274]

I consulted the 1910 U.S. Census to see if I could trace Howard Skinner's whereabouts further back in time. The 1910 census registered him in the same household as his parents—Milton and Ella Skinner—who had nine children. They owned their farm and their son, Howard, age twenty-two, was a farmhand. The 1910 census gives no street names or route numbers; therefore, it is impossible to tell exactly where they lived. However, they did live in the vicinity of our farmhouse because the Coffenberger family was one of their near neighbors according to the census.[275] The 1883 tax map shows that the Coffenbergers owned farm property on nearby Trough Road, but it does not show a Skinner farm. The Skinners must have bought their place sometime after 1883.

---

273 *Shepherdstown Register*, Shepherdstown, W.Va., July 13, 1922, 1. LOC Chronicling America.

274 1920 U.S. Census, record of Howard T. Skinner household. Retrieved from https://www.familysearch.org/ark:/61903/3:1:33SQ-GRJC-95Y?i=29&wc=QZJY -L5C%3A1037175801%2C1036713301%2C1038350001%2C1589332459&cc=1488411

275 1910 U.S. Census, record of Howard T. Skinner household. Retrieved from https://www.familysearch.org/ark:/61903/3:1:33SQ-GYY2-W6T?i=19&cc=1727033

I will digress a little before continuing with more information about the Skinners' Selby farm tenancy. A frightening accident befell Howard Skinner in 1915 when the *Shepherdstown Register* reported that he was badly scalded while helping Luther Thomson butcher hogs near town. He was pulling a hog to the scalding tub when he slipped and fell into the hot water. He scalded one shoulder and one hip—part of his skin coming off in the process of removing his clothing. The article described it as "a narrow escape from a dreadful death."[276] His wife must have done a commendable job nursing him back to health. He lived forty-seven more years before his death in 1962. A 1917 article reported that Howard Skinner was leaving the George W. Osborn farm and moving to George M. Knott's farm at Molers Crossroads.[277] Hence, we know the Skinners managed several other farms before settling at the Selby farm.

Charles F. Byers placed his last lumber ad from the Selby farm on April 8, 1920. I believe he left the farm soon after, allowing time for the Skinners to move into the farmhouse and to be counted there in the 1920 census.

The next news story about Howard Skinner appeared in 1922 when the *Shepherdstown Register* reported that E. E. Harwood threshed Skinner's wheat crop, which yielded about fifteen bushels per acre.[278] The 1930 U.S. Census recorded that the Skinners married at ages twenty-three and eighteen. It listed Howard Skinner as head-of-household at age forty-two with his wife, Mary, and six children ages seven to fourteen. They were still living in the same location as in 1920 and still renting our farm.

I believe the family's increasing number of children, supported by the 1930 census, helps explain the house's 1929 addition. We also learn from the 1930 census that the house had no "radio set," possibly because it had yet to receive electricity. The year 1930 was the only year the national head count asked

276 *Shepherdstown Register*, Shepherdstown, W.Va., December 2, 1915, 3. LOC Chronicling America.
277 *Shepherdstown Register*, Shepherdstown, W.Va., March 29, 1917, 3. LOC Chronicling America.
278 *Shepherdstown Register*, Shepherdstown, W.Va., July 6, 1922, 3. LOC Chronicling America.

this question. Lastly, this census tells us all family members could read, but the parents did not have advanced schooling, meaning high school.[279]

In 1940, the U.S. Census counted Howard Skinner as head-of-household at age fifty-two with his wife, M. Lorraine, and three children: John T., William M., and Howard T. Jr.—twenty-one, eighteen, and seventeen years old. They were still living in the same location and renting our farm. Howard T. Skinner Sr. was the farm operator. His son, John, had a seventh-grade education and was a carpenter in construction work at a stone quarry.[280] The older children must have left home by 1940.

The Skinners rented our farm for twenty-six years before finally buying it in 1946 from Florence Williamson Sampson Clarke. When Mary L. Skinner, in turn, sold it in 1969, the Skinner family became the longest tenured occupants of the farmhouse in its history—a duration of forty-nine years. I will continue their story a little further in Chapter 9 about the recent resident owners of the property.

But first, I will return to the earliest days of the farm to consider the euphemistically-named "peculiar institution." In the next chapter, we will explore the history of slavery at the George Morgan farm from its establishment until the Civil War. This period includes the time when George Morgan, his wife and heirs, and John Sigler occupied the farmhouse.

---

279 1930 U.S. Census, record of Howard T. Skinner household. Retrieved from https://www.familysearch.org/ark:/61903/3:1:33S7-9RZP-G8J?i=12&wc=QZFW-L9B%3A648804101%2C649117201%2C649139301%2C1589282323&cc=1810731

280 1940 U.S. Census, record of Howard T. Skinner household. Retrieved from https://www.familysearch.org/ark:/61903/3:1:3QS7-L9M1-YQXQ?i=1&wc=QZFM-KXB%3A794518101%2C790172601%2C796956201%2C952288801&cc=2000219

CHAPTER 8 SLAVERY AT THE FARM

DID SLAVES EVER live and work on George Morgan's and later Walter Selby's farm? This question is not easy to answer. Nothing in the JFH Papers, the local media, or recorded deeds helps us solve this puzzle. We have seen no evidence of a slave quarter on the property. The only resources that offer any potential for learning whether slaves toiled in our fields are an 1800 tax list and the early U.S. censuses.[281]

The British Army destroyed the original 1790 and 1800 U.S. Census schedules for Virginia when it occupied Washington, D.C., in August 1814. These early records named the heads-of-households and counted the number of inhabitants, including slaves, in each family. Only abstracts containing the number of inhabitants of each county survive. This misfortune ensures that we will not find any direct evidence of slavery at the farm from these documents. Local census information from a number of counties collected between 1782 and 1785 is available on microfilm at the Library of Virginia. However, the names of these counties are not available on the library's website, and they may not include Jefferson County. Weighing the effort required to discover relevant evidence against the chances of finding it, I decided not to pursue this source material. Nonetheless, the 1800 property tax list for Berkeley County and the U.S. Census records from 1810 to 1860 do offer help.

The ensuing discussion maintains a chronological sequence matching farm owners and tenants with tax list and census years. It explores what we can learn and extrapolate about slavery at the farm from the scanty records available.

1800 Property Tax List and 1810 Census

George Morgan's heirs were his widow, Drusilla, and their children William, Van, Raleigh, and Lydia. Drusilla married Azariah Thornburg (1768–1807) on August 18, 1798.[282] After remarrying, she and her new

---

281 1790 Virginia Census (VA-NOTES). Retrieved from http://www.lva.virginia.gov/public/guides/va2_1790census.htm

282 Virginia Marriages, 1785-1940. Retrieved from https://www.familysearch.org/ark:/61903/1:1:XRVV-SJQ

husband in all probability lived at her farmhouse. She would have inherited it from George Morgan, although he did not record a will. At some point, her children took ownership of the farm, and they did not fully sell it out of the family until 1817. After Azariah's death in 1807, Drusilla probably had no reason to leave her farm. The 1810 census essentially supports this premise by listing some of her near neighbors' family names as Taylor, Hendricks, Moler, and Show—all names historically associated with the area surrounding the farmhouse. I will explain shortly why I believe Drusilla remained at the farm as late as 1817. I have put forward where I think Azariah and Drusilla lived for the purpose of connecting any slaves they owned to their home place.

The Berkeley County property tax list of 1800 notes that Azariah Thornburg owned two slaves—one between twelve and sixteen and the other over sixteen.[283] The 1810 census reveals that widow Drusilla Thornburg was the head of her household and had six slaves.[284] If Azariah and Drusilla Thornburg owned two slaves in 1800 and the widowed Drusilla—still living at the farmhouse— owned six slaves in 1810, it is likely that slaves had been part of our farm's way of life since its beginning. The addition of four slaves to this household between 1800 and 1810 might have stemmed from inheritance, acquisition, or procreation.

A larger question is why Drusilla lived in a simple log house if she could afford to maintain six slaves without a husband. A majority of the area's residents did not own slaves, and of those who did, owning six slaves was above the average based on a cursory review of the data presented on a few of the 1810 census's pages before and after the one listing Drusilla. Walter Selby, one of the most prosperous men in Shepherdstown, owned only five slaves in 1810, according to the same record. It is possible that Drusilla's farm produced enough to support her family as well as the slaves, who no doubt lived in austere conditions. Another possibility is that Drusilla hired some of her slaves out to other farms.

The 1810 census records the name of a George Morgan heir twice— William Morgan. Neither of these two William Morgans seems to have been living at the farmhouse based on the names of their near neighbors

---

283 Berkeley County Property Tax List of 1800, transcribed version, BCHS archives.
284 United States Census, 1810, image 362. Retrieved from https://www.familysearch
.org/ark:/61903/3:1:33S7-9YB4-D27?i=361&cc=1803765

in the census. The elder of the two was too old to be George Morgan's offspring—he was forty-five or older. He might be Colonel William Morgan's son Zacheus's son, who would be George Morgan's cousin—see Deed No. 10. The younger William could have been a George Morgan heir—he is listed in the twenty-six to forty-five year old age range. He had no slaves, and he may have died before the first partial sale of the farm to Walter Selby in 1811. If he were George Morgan's son, his demise could explain why he was not a grantor on any of the three deeds transferring the property to Selby over several years like each of his three siblings were.

George Morgan's son, Raleigh (aka Rawleigh Jr.), sold his one-third interest in the farmhouse property to Walter Selby in 1811 (Deed No. 8). None of Drusilla's children's names appear in the 1810 census indicating they did not head their own households. All or some of them may have lived with their mother at the farmhouse at the time. The 1810 census names only the heads-of-households and counts the number of others in the home. Since the 1811 sale was solely for a one-third interest in the property, this transaction might have allowed the residents to remain.

Van Morgan sold his one-third interest in the farm to Walter Selby in 1815 (Deed No. 14), the same year Drusilla married her third husband— Charles Williams. Since Walter Selby did not purchase the final one-third interest in the farm until 1817 (Deed No. 15), from Lydia Morgan McCauley, Charles and Drusilla could have lived on at the farm until then. We know that John Sigler became the tenant manager of the farm in 1818, perhaps a sign that Drusilla had moved away by that time. However, knowing that she held slaves in 1810, we can judge that she still had some at the farm until she left, which likely was around 1817 or 1818.

1820 Census

The 1820 census lists both John Sigler Jr. and John Sigler Sr. Given their census age ranges, John Jr. would have been the one who tenanted our farmhouse beginning in 1818. Since the names are in alphabetical order in this census's schedules, it is impossible to place where he lived based on nearby neighbors' names. We are fortunate to have his son Michael's obituary, mentioned in the previous chapter, to tell us that John Sigler undertook tenanting of our farm in 1818. The 1820 census only gives us his name, the age ranges of the eight members of his family, and that he had no slaves.

Although John Sigler had no slaves, he had two sons between ten and twenty years old who could have worked the farm in addition to Sarah, his wife.[285] He could also have hired slaves from others, which was a familiar practice. Walter Selby's household had four slaves in 1820, but none worked in agriculture. These facts imply that Selby's slaves did not typically work at his farm, but this would not have prevented him from sending some over to help with the field work occasionally. After all, we have seen his 1815 ad in Figure 5.8 offering to sell a slave suitable for farm work.

Drusilla Thornburg's name appears in this census, and it seems that she was living in the same general neighborhood as she was in 1810 judging by the names of some of her neighbors. If she had left the farm by 1818 when John Sigler is known to have taken it over, she could have moved to a nearby house and still had many of the same neighbors she had in 1810. The census lists her in the forty-five and above age range. Her household includes three free males between sixteen and forty-five and one male slave.[286] The free men were most likely her sons or even lodgers, but not her third husband, Charles Williams. He would have been older, and his absence hints that he might be deceased. I cannot explain why Drusilla would go by her second husband's name in 1820. Drusilla Morgan Thornburg no longer appears in Virginia censuses after 1820. However, she is the grantor of an 1824 deed (No. 21) releasing her dower right in the 200-acre farm Walter Selby bought from her children over multiple years. She was living in Washington County, Maryland, in 1824.

1830 Census

As in the 1820 census, the 1830 census records no slaves in John Sigler's household. However, he had two sons between ten and twenty-six years of age plus a daughter between ten and fifteen.[287] All of these offspring and

---

285 United States Census, 1820. Retrieved from https://www.familysearch.org/ark:/61903/3:1:33S7-9YYY-SJF?i=3&cc=1803955

286 United States Census, 1820. Retrieved from https://www.familysearch.org/ark:/61903/1:1:XHLZ-412

287 United States Census, 1830. Retrieved from https://www.familysearch.org/ark:/61903/3:1:33SQ-GYYK-3SHG?i=61&cc=1803958

John's wife were doubtless capable of helping with the farm work. Temporarily employing slaves was still an option for Sigler in 1830. Walter Selby had one older male slave and three young female slaves according to the 1830 census, but none worked in agriculture. However, this would not preclude him from allowing some of his slaves to work for John Sigler as already noted.

In 1832, Walter Selby together with Samuel Deitrick purchased four slaves (Deed No. 22)—Harry, Aley, Thornton, and Ann—and a variety of household articles from J. R. Douglas for $1,995. The title to these people's very beings, already cited in Chapter 6, says "[t]o have and to hold the aforesaid slaves and their increase of the families thereof, and the other movable property above described." Movable property—a horrific comparison for fellow human beings. Could Walter Selby have sent some of these people over to work in our fields?

1840–1860 Censuses

I could not find John Sigler listed in any of the census schedules from 1840 through 1860. However, it is realistic to conclude that he held no slaves throughout this period based on his earlier census information. He would also have had older children in the household through most of this period, and his wife was still living—all able to work around the farm. Walter Selby had only one older female slave in 1840, but it is unlikely that he would have sent her to the farm, needing her for domestic work at his home.[288] By 1850, Walter Selby had three slaves—a fifteen-year-old male, twenty-six-year-old female, and a sixty-year-old female. He could have sent the younger of these slaves to work on the farm periodically.

By 1860, Walter Selby had passed away and his son, Henry, became head of the Wynkoop Tavern household as reported in the census of that year. The 1860 slave census is not freely accessible on the internet today. However, I retrieved information about it formerly located on the *wvgeohistory.com* website, which indicated that Henry had no slaves. Unfortunately, this website is no longer searchable for this type of material. If we think about the 1867 photograph in Figure 5.9 showing Mami Sally, the family might have freed her before the 1860 slave census if she had been with the family back then. This rendering could account for Henry not owning any slaves in 1860.

---

288 United States Census, 1840. Retrieved from https://www.familysearch.org /ark:/61903/3:1:33SQ-GYBM-SPP?i=13&cc=1786457

We can conclude that our farm did exploit involuntary African American labor roughly from 1780 through 1818. But after that year, it looks like the farm did not hold slaves who were continuously bonded to the tenant and the land. We resume our story about the farmhouse's owners and dwellers in the next chapter.

CHAPTER 9 RECENT RESIDENT OWNERS

I PRESENT SIX twentieth-century and twenty-first-century deeds and a will in Appendix B. They recount the chain of ownership of the farmhouse toward the end of the Selby and Hamtramck family lines to the present. I have numbered them sequentially with those in Appendix A. In this chapter, I offer a summary of what I know about the tenure of each owner who followed Florence Williamson Sampson Clarke.

Howard T. and Mary L. Skinner 1946–1969

On June 18, 1946, Florence Williamson Sampson Clarke granted Howard T. (1887–1962) and Mary L. (1895–1991) Skinner, a tract of land called Wheatland farm south of Shepherdstown containing about 275 acres. This ownership transfer (Deed No. 33) ended the log farmhouse's continuous ownership by Walter B. Selby and his descendants from 1811 through 1946, a period of 135 years. Nevertheless, this deed was not an arm's-length transaction, the consideration being only ten dollars. This incongruity leaves the question of what was the nature of the relationship between Florence W. S. Clarke and the Skinners to cause her effectively to give the property to them.

In Chapter 7, we learned that the Skinners had been tenants at the farm for twenty-six years before this purchase. If the Skinners had a lease-to-own agreement with Florence W. S. Clarke, I could understand why she might have sold it to them for ten dollars. If the Skinner's had built the 1929 addition with their own funds, I would have another reason to believe this.

There are several Skinners now living in Jefferson and Berkeley Counties. There is also a Skinner law firm and a Skinner construction company in Charles Town where I hoped to find a descendant. I contacted all of them but found no one with knowledge of the Skinners' ownership of our house.

Gilbert Page Wright Jr. 1969–2001

Widow Mary L. Skinner and others granted Gilbert P. Wright Jr. a significant part of the tract of land south of Shepherdstown called Wheatland farm by Deed No. 34 on March 12, 1969. This transfer excluded two tracts amounting to about 29 ¼ acres of the original 275-acre Wheatland farm, which existed during Florence Williamson Sampson

Clarke's ownership. Nonetheless, the remaining 246 acres included the log farmhouse. I do not know how the grantors, besides Mary L. Skinner, came to their part-ownership of the property; however, some of them are evidently Skinner family members.

Page Wright kept a large dairy herd and later a beef herd at the farm according to area residents who knew him. He also raised corn and alfalfa. Wright hosted various training events for 4-H, Future Farmers of America, and college students. He added several large modern barns to his property. An aerial photograph of the farm taken in 1999 shows all the buildings existing at that time. Page Wright was a graduate of Shepherdstown High School and a lifelong farmer. He was born in Martinsburg, served in the Korean War, and died in 2010 at the age of seventy-eight.[289]

Mark Mulligan and David R. Haarberg 2001–2011

On March 13, 2001, Gilbert P. and Stacy Wright granted Mark Mulligan and David R. Haarberg a parcel described as the 10.1999-acre Lot No. 1 of the Gilbert and Stacy Wright Minor Subdivision. Jefferson County Plat Book No. 18 contains a plan of Lot No. 1. This parcel includes the log farmhouse. The Wrights subdivided a substantial part of their 246-acre property at the time of this transfer. The resulting development—Wrights Field—now encompasses twenty-two sizable colonial-style homes. Mark Mulligan and David Haarberg finished extensive renovations and restorations to the log farmhouse, which I will describe in Chapter 10. Farming effectively ceased under their ownership, given the drastically reduced acreage of the property. Still, these owners kept a few goats in a fenced area for brush control.

Joseph and Lynne F. Goss 2011–Present

On June 3, 2011, Mark Mulligan and David R. Haarberg granted Lynne and me the same tract and log farmhouse conveyed to them by the Wrights. We built a major addition to it in 2013, which I will describe in the next chapter. We also resumed some modest agriculture by permitting neighbors to mow hay and graze horses, calves, and goats on the pasture.

---

289 Wright, Gilbert Page Jr., "Book of Memories." Retrieved from http://www.brownfuneralhomeswv.com/book-of-memories/1357398/Wright-Gilbert/view-condolences.php

Todd Banks is the current operator of our farming activity, which consists of transporting several calves from his adjoining farm to graze on our pasture in summer and mowing and baling hay to help feed his main herd. He also installed piping and a trough for our visiting cattle, which fills from a well near the antique bank barn on his property. This historic barn used to belong to earlier owners of our farmhouse. In a way, this pipeline reconnects our homestead with some of its original farmland, which Page Wright sold in 2001.

CHAPTER 10 ARCHITECTURAL DIARY

ORIGINALLY BUILT OF chestnut oak logs harvested from the land and stones quarried on site, the George Morgan House has undergone enormous changes over its 238 years. The oldest part of the house measures about twenty feet wide by twenty-six feet long, has two floors, a basement, and a walk-up attic. An early owner could have added the second floor to the house—a possibility I will discuss shortly.

The log core of the house has only two bays today, but this element might have been different at the time of construction. A bay is an architectural element that corresponds to the space defined by a window or door opening on a façade. If a building has more than one story, the bays usually align vertically on all floors. The east interior wall of the farmhouse's first floor shows unmistakable evidence of log in-fill where a door existed between two windows, which would have constituted a third bay.

There was no symmetry to the original fenestration on the first floor or the alignment of windows between the first and second floors—an unusual condition I cannot explain. Not surprisingly, the door and window openings on the east basement wall do not align with former or current doors and windows on the floors above. The position of the original doors and windows is indeed extremely confusing.

There is a single chimney on the north wall of the log core. Neither the basement stonework nor the exposed first-floor logs suggest that there was ever another chimney on the south wall. I believe this feature expresses the house's simple beginnings. The original stone cooking hearth that appears in Figure 9.1 still remains on the north basement wall. Basement hearths are not usually seen in houses built after about 1815 according to John Allen.[290]

Floor Plans

I know little about the house's earliest floor plans. None of the existing floorboards is original. All the original interior walls or partitions that might have existed on the first floor are gone. Nearly all of the early farmhouses in Jefferson County matched one of three basic floor plans—

---

290 Allen, 122.

center-hall, side-hall, or hall-and-parlor.[291] We can safely rule out the center-hall plan for the modest George Morgan House because it required more space than the house afforded and it represented the least common of these three plans in the 1780's according to John Allen's survey.[292]

FIGURE 10.1 Basement stone cooking hearth. *Credit: Joseph Goss.*

A side-hall plan would seem to be a strong candidate for the original layout of the house because of its compact and efficient nature and the need for a chimney at only one end. Still, the side-hall plan was not common among the homes of the 1780's that Allen surveyed.[293] Side-hall houses needed only one chimney, as the hall was narrow and not intended as living space. Hence, the hall area did not need a fireplace. If the farmhouse's one-time door now filled in with logs was to serve as the entrance to a side hall, it was too far from the south end of the house to make sense for a side-hall plan. This plan would have created a side hall that was too wide with unneeded windows in an unheated space.

Wealthier early settlers generally favored hall-and-parlor style houses with at least three bays and built of durable stone. However, a few log houses also used this plan. This design was the most common house plan of the 1780's among those surveyed by Allen. The hall-and-parlor consists of two rooms of unequal size on the main floor, a plan that came down from post medieval house designs in England. The larger of the two rooms, the hall, included the entry door with a chimney on the end wall. It afforded space for the household's activities of daily living. A partition separated the smaller room, the parlor, from the hall and another partition sometimes

---

291 Allen, 36.

292 Allen, 75.

293 Allen, 75.

divided this space into two rooms. This room was usually, but not always, appointed with another chimney on the end wall opposite the hall chimney. Eighteenth-century inventories found parlor rooms furnished with books, beds, desks, and more elegant furniture revealing their functions.[294],[295]

According to my reading of the physical traces of earlier door and window positions in the house's log core, the original house followed a hall-and-parlor floor plan. The inhabitants might not have thought heat to be essential for the activities that took place in the unheated parlors. Refer to the implied original arrangement of the farmhouse in Figure 9.2 to better understand this. The George Morgan House might not have conformed to

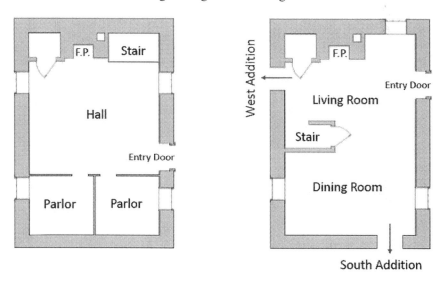

FIGURE 10.2 Inferred original hall-and-parlor plan and present-day plan. *Credit: Joseph Goss and Eric D Goss.*

any of the plan types described here. The first floor could have been a one-room space enclosed by four log walls called a single pen or crib.[296] This floor plan might solve the puzzle of how the occupants heated the

---

294 Allen, 75.

295 Allen, 38.

296 Bomberger, Bruce D., "The Preservation and Repair of Historic Log Buildings, Preservations Briefs 26,"Technical Preservation Services, National Park Service. Retrieved from http://www.nps.gov/tps/how-to-preserve/briefs/26-log-buildings .htm#damages

whole house by a sole end-wall fireplace. A view of the house's log core appears in Figure 9.3, revealing the open floor plan it exhibits today.

Stairs

The house's original staircase is gone, replaced by a newer, comparatively large, fully enclosed staircase with a midstair landing and ninety-degree turn. It is close to the center of the west wall of the structure making for an awkward division of space today. The original stair would have been quite narrow, spiral-like, and tucked into a corner next to the chimney as was typical for the period.[297]

FIGURE 10.3 Log core of the farmhouse, 2017. *Credit: Joseph Goss.*

Reading the logs on the chimney wall reveals that the window to the right of the chimney is not original. It was cut into the wall following the removal of the corner stair. A mill-sawed beam spans the ceiling above the former corner stair unlike all the other massive hand-hewn ceiling beams. This beam supports the upstairs floorboards where the corner-stair opening provided access to the second floor. This formulation favors the house including the second floor from the beginning. One could still argue that the house lacked the second floor at the time of construction and that the stair accessed an attic above the first floor. However, the limited headspace above a corner stair that would have been near an eave of the

---

297 Allen, 38.

house makes this argument less convincing. Of course, the corner stair itself could have been added when a second floor materialized.

The space in the basement directly below the former corner stair is significant. This space exhibits a squared-off hand-hewn beam in the ceiling, which supports the main-level flooring. All the other timbers in the basement ceiling are enormous unhewn logs. Indeed, the squared-off beam did not need to be as stout as the others as it spans a much shorter distance between the stone hearth and the exterior basement wall. The hand-hewn quality of this beam suggests it is part of the original fabric of the house, which could cast doubt on the corner stair theory.

Thinking it through more carefully, someone might have removed part of one of the squared-off ceiling beams supporting the second floor to make way for the new stair. Recognizing that the removed section of the beam could have gone to the basement, I measured the cross-section of the remaining piece of the partly-removed beam. Its dimensions matched precisely those of the squared-off beam in the basement, and the other first-floor ceiling beams did not match it.

Another clue that helps confirm the borrowed-beam concept is that the removed beam was longer than needed to fashion the closure beam used in the basement to support the new floorboards above it. Furthermore, nothing in the basement space below this beam would have blocked a stair. Based on this evidence, it is certain the house initially included a corner stair in the location I have described.

Construction Details

The foundation and basement walls are of stone construction. The house banks into a hill and faces east with its back to the weather. This style came from Pennsylvania where many early Shepherdstown settlers originated. The chimney is inboard and built of stone up to the top of the basement wall but built of brick from the first floor to its cap. The brickwork of the fireplace and chimney on the first floor appear to be original. Since the first commercial brick kiln in Shepherdstown did not begin operation until the mid-1790's, I was puzzled about how George Morgan could have obtained bricks for his chimney around 1780. Todd Funkhouser of BCHS explained to me that people made their own bricks on-site before the opening of commercial kilns in the area. This custom might have been the case with our house.[298] There is plenty of clay on the property for brick making. Another distinctive aspect of the chimney is that it features clay mortar instead of cement mortar.

There are three fireplaces in the house—one on each floor counting the basement cooking hearth. Previous owners sealed the opening of the second-floor fireplace. The first-floor fireplace accommodates an up-to-date wood-stove insert and is the only one still in service.

The exposed interior log walls and ceiling beams of the log crib show the adze marks of hand hewing. I wonder whether this sort of craftsmanship was the exclusive province of professional housewrights, or if it was an ordinary skill. I suspect housewrights did not build our farmhouse, given the seemingly random nature of some of its original architectural elements.

An underground cylindrical concrete cistern on the east side of the house once connected to a long-abandoned roof gutter system. You can still see a pipe penetration through the cistern's concrete top slab, which received rainwater from a gutter downspout. The cistern's location steps from the basement kitchen must have been convenient.

Additions and Alterations

The first addition to the house came in the early or mid-nineteenth century.[299] It consists of a twelve-foot wide two-story wood-frame structure spanning the length of the house's south wall. It gives the house the appearance of having three bays. The builder opened doorways between the original log structure and the addition on both floors and built steep, narrow staircases into one end of the extension from the first floor to the attic.

There is no evidence of how this addition obtained heat, although wood or coal stoves might have been the most practical means. The tenants I cited in Chapter 7 confirm this idea reasonably well by the stoves listed in their auction advertisements in the 1870's. This addition sits on a stone foundation and dirt-floor crawl space. During a visit to the house, architectural historian John Allen observed that window and door trim

---

298 Funkhouser, R. Todd, personal communication, BCHS, June 4, 2015.
299 Haarberg, David, written communication, March 3, 2011.

throughout the original log house and the nineteenth-century south addition was Greek Revival in style dating from about 1840.[300] This kind of trim was not present in the original house since it had not yet come into fashion. I conclude that the Greek Revival trim, depicted in Figure 9.4, was a trend-conscious upgrade added to the entire house at the time of the south extension. Using this logic, the date of the addition itself could be about 1840.

The need for the addition could have been to accommodate a growing tenant family. We learned in Chapter 7 that the tenant at this time was John Sigler. Since the oldest of John and Sarah Sigler's six or seven children was born in 1818 and the youngest in 1832 according to the 1850 census, I am tempted to push the date of the addition—presumed built around 1840—back in time. This notion would suggest the window and door trim might have been put in some years after the addition itself. Still, it seems like a needless luxury to upgrade the house with new interior trim throughout only to keep it in style for the tenant family.

FIGURE 10.4 Greek Revival interior wood trim. *Credit: Joseph Goss.*

As I discussed in Chapter 7, the tenants might have served more like hired farm managers than poor farmers. Thus, the owner at the time of the south addition's construction, Walter B. Selby, might have used the farmhouse as an incentive to keep a capable tenant manager at the farm. The addition and new trim may have been installed to accomplish this goal.

---

300 Allen, personal communication, February 10, 2012.

I do not think the house initially received exterior siding because a small area of the original unclad exterior is visible inside the attic stairwell of the circa 1840 south addition. This area shows exposed logs and daubing and chinking with some of the old whitewash paint still intact. Old weathered German lap-clapboard siding completely covers the exterior of the house today. I believe the house got its siding at the time of the south addition, whose wood-frame structure had to be protected. Another clue pointing to this conclusion is that the old siding around the whole log structure and south addition is all of a piece. There is no discontinuity in the cladding at the joints between these two sections of the house.

Owners of log houses often covered them with siding to harmonize a new addition with the whole. This practice was especially vital if the original core and its extension were of different types of construction such as log and wood frame.[301] I believe this one upgrade did more to save the George Morgan House from gradual ruin than any other improvement.

The south addition to the log house might have generated improvements besides siding and Greek Revival trim. These might have included new windows, doors, interior walls, floorboards, the new main stairway, and removal of the old spiral stair next to the fireplace. An entirely new attic-roof frame materialized along with the south extension, as revealed by the continuous unitary structure it now forms running the entire length of the building.

The only major twentieth-century change to the George Morgan House was a two-story wood-frame addition. It rests on a poured-concrete foundation and forms the west wing of the structure. As mentioned in Chapter 5, this addition dates from 1929. There was once an entry porch on the north side of this extension. A door-entry cut is still visible in the baseboard beneath one of its windows.

The window and door trim in the 1929 addition is a simplified version of the Greek Revival trim in the older parts of the house. It presents the same kind of corner blocks and sills but lacks the multi layered effect of the earlier headers and jambs seen in Figure 9.4.

---

301 Bomberger.

Stoves on both levels heated this addition, suggested by filled-in stovepipe openings on an inboard brick chimney on the west wall. Former owners wrote that there might have been other attached structures on the east side of the house—such as porches and a summer kitchen—but there is no physical evidence of their presence.[302]

Gilbert Wright built a porch running the full length of the east façade of the house in the 1970's or 1980's. The new porch accommodated two doors into the house. Most likely it replaced the earlier entry porch on the north side of the 1929 expansion.

In 2004 or 2005, David Haarberg and Mark Mulligan undertook an extensive renovation of the house. This work included removing the plaster on the first-floor walls to expose the logs. It also included removing the plaster ceiling on the first floor to reveal the hand-hewn beams above. When they took ownership, all the walls and ceilings were plastered. A friend mentioned that they had not recognized the log-built nature of the house until they saw the exposed logs in the attic stairwell.

Nail holes for the lath boards above the plaster ceiling and plaster ghosting between the removed lath boards are still visible on the underside of the ceiling beams. Traces of old plaster applied to the log walls and the brick chimney remain discernible. The interior logs and beams of eighteenth-century log houses received plaster covering for some of the same reasons the exteriors received siding—insulation, ease of maintenance, appearance, and keeping out vermin.[303] The rustic exposed-log look is rarely historically correct, however much it suits contemporary tastes. In any case, it creates the cave-like atmosphere of the farmhouse's log core.

Owners Haarberg and Mulligan completely renovated the kitchen on the first floor in the nineteenth-century south addition. To accommodate this work, they moved a door on the east wall to the south wall of the extension. They also thoroughly renovated a bathroom on the second floor. I applaud these owners for their extensive renovation of the house, for reinforcing it structurally, and employing period finishes and fixtures for modern necessities. They also installed extensive new mechanical-electrical systems and energy conserving improvements such as up-to-date

302 Haarberg.
303 Bomberger.

high-efficiency windows. They have done the most of any owners since at least the early or mid-1800's to preserve this historic structure and ensure its survival long into the future.

In 2012, we began to plan an extensive one-story addition on the south side of the farmhouse. We hired architect Dirk DeVault of Limn Studio in Hagerstown, Maryland, to design the structure and Elk Branch Builders, Inc., to build it. Curtis Keesecker of Elk Branch was the superintendent for the project, which began construction in spring 2013. Our friend, George Hoover, an independent master carpenter and house builder, did all the custom interior finish work, such as flooring, door and window trim, cabinetry, and tile work. His daughter, Ann, assisted him and accomplished substantial parts of the work herself. The Hoovers completed their work by the end of 2013. The addition is of wood-frame construction built on a concrete block foundation. It includes a master bedroom with connected bathroom and closet, a laundry room, half bathroom, entry hall, coat closet, and an attached two-bay garage.

We borrowed several architectural details from older sections of the house for the 2013 addition. These details included replicating the door and window trim from the 1929 addition. The medicine cabinets in the master bathroom are custom-built replicas of the existing antique medicine cabinet in the second-floor bathroom. We used antique doors and nineteenth-century surface rim locks with ceramic knobs throughout the interior. We bought most of the doors but found one in the barn and rescued one from the goat shed. George Hoover found hand-hewn beams from a collapsing barn in the area to install as a decorative element on the ceiling of the entry hall—echoing the exposed beams in the original log core of the house.

The 2013 project also included the replacement and extension of the structurally unsound porch on the east side of the house. We chose horizontal porch rails because of the historical precursors of this pattern we observed on several old homes in Jefferson and nearby Loudoun Counties in addition to their visual appeal. We matched the existing historical siding with new German lap-clapboard siding to shroud the entire addition.

Another part of this project consisted of building a stair from the first floor to the basement. When we moved in, there was no way to access the basement except to go outside and enter it through an exterior door. This situation was inconvenient in the extreme at night and in inclement weather. It took us a long time to figure out what to do about this obstacle since there was no room to build a conventional staircase that would not conflict with some structural or mechanical element in the basement.

Driving out to the house from Maryland one day, the solution struck us—cut a trap door into the floor of the 1929 addition and build a steep stair beneath it. There was a perfect place for this door in front of a wall of built-in book shelving with no obstructions below. The bookshelves guaranteed that no heavy furniture would be placed on the floor in front of it. We gave George Hoover a set of plans drawn by Dirk DeVault and he built a masterpiece of carpentry. He cut the trap door out of the existing wood flooring and it is nearly invisible. It has become a tourist attraction for all our visitors.

Outbuildings and Grounds

No historic outbuildings remain on the present-day 10.2-acre farm property. However, there is an old heavily cracked and deteriorated concrete slab foundation about twelve-feet wide by twenty-feet long a few yards upstream of the pond. I have been unable to learn what sort of building stood on the foundation even though area residents remember seeing a wooden structure there years ago. Some suggest that it could have been a piggery, a corn crib, a wash house, or a whiskey stillhouse. I admit it is a stretch, but I like the whiskey still suggestion. It fits in well with the unsolved 1814 stillhouse robbery at the farm and Latrobe's journal entry about the insobriety of rural folk—excluding our farmhouse tenants of course. Moreover, flowing water was only steps away.

I have found no remnants of a slave quarter on the property. Remains of a quarter serving the Selby farm, if any ever existed, could be beyond the boundaries of the current property making them difficult to find or access. Construction of the adjoining Wrights Field subdivision could also have destroyed it.

There is a small collapsed frame house directly across Engle Molers Road from our property, which could have been a house for the farm's laborers. It was never on the farm's property and it was almost certainly never a slave quarter. Someone might have built it after the Civil War to house emancipated slaves who may have worked at our farm or others nearby. I noted this possibility in Chapter 7 during William F. Myers' tenancy.

The primary source of water for the house has been a surface spring for many years. The current spring is at the bottom of the hill the house stands on and is next to a stream, which feeds a man-made pond. A small concrete-block structure covers the spring and houses a submersible pump and pressure-equalizing tank. There is an older spring nearby downstream of the active spring. Its concrete foundation is still visible and its constant flow emits a soothing sound whenever we pass it.

Page Wright told Haarberg and Mulligan that the farm's spring was one of the few springs and wells in the area that did not fail in the drought of the 1930's.[304] Wright might have heard this report from the Skinners who lived in the house in the 1930's and sold it to him. In 2012, I found a heavily corroded age-old pump discarded near the spring house. It probably dates from the first half of the twentieth century, which suggests the age of the present spring house.[305]

Haarberg and Mulligan built a modern metal-sided thirty-foot by forty-foot pole barn on the property. It replaced a much smaller wooden structure on the same site, which is indistinctly visible in the 1999 aerial photograph. We found a few rotted boards from the old structure at the base of a wall of the new barn. The modern barn appears on a 2004 aerial photograph of the property, confirming its construction between 2001 and 2004.

These owners created an extensive system of mowed walking trails throughout the property, which we have maintained. They even laid out an eighty-foot diameter seven-circuit classical labyrinth in the lawn on the west side of the house, which we have attempted to save.

Noticing that we had an enormous tree on the back side of the property, I contacted the West Virginia Division of Forestry to see if it might merit listing in the state Big Trees Program. A forester came out to measure it in June 2018 and identified it as a hackberry tree. He reported that it could be the third or fourth largest hackberry in West Virginia and is under

---

304 Haarberg.
305 Hoover, George R., personal communication, December 11, 2015.

consideration for listing.[306] At the time of this writing, I have not heard of a decision.

A seasonal spring-fed stream runs through the property discharging into a sizable man-made pond. This basin hosts several large and colorful koi, whose offspring regularly attract great blue herons. Alarmingly, it also houses an unknown number of vicious snapping turtles, which have decided several times to wander up past the house perhaps in search of a new pond or, salmon-like, to the nest of their hatching. There is a smaller pond nearby on the Aspen Pool farm—conceivably the target of our wandering snappers. These nomads may be part of what the previous owners called a wildlife exchange program between the ponds.

Page Wright installed the pond in the 1980's under a U.S. Department of Agriculture conservation program. It discharges into a deep sinkhole. Springs and sinkholes are characteristic of the karst geological formation, which much of the Eastern Panhandle overlays. Karst consists of limestone or other soluble rock replete with voids, caverns, and underground streams.

And this brings us up-to-date with the physical changes to the George Morgan House and farm over its 238-year history. Who can imagine what kinds of changes it might see in its next 238 years?

---

306 Williamson, Tyler, email communication, June 18, 2018.

CHAPTER 11 CLOSING THOUGHTS

O NE NOTABLE OBSERVATION from my research is that the descendants who followed the early pioneers connected with our farmhouse did not leave as great a mark as their forebears. Perhaps this was because the first settlers had already tamed the wilderness and broken free from British rule leaving their offspring with diminished potential to achieve recognition. Furthermore, the pioneers had so many children that they had considerably more competition for prominence.

I make an exception for Colonel John F. Hamtramck who served worthily as Osage Indian agent and as a distinguished officer in the War with Mexico. I also make an exception for the dauntless service of the unremembered men and women of Shepherdstown, and doubtless the occupants of our farmhouse, who cared for the wounded and dying from the Battle of Antietam. Selby and Hamtramck family members surely made the same sacrifices at the Wynkoop Tavern.

If we still seem to know too little about the early Morgan and Selby owners of our house, we know even less about their enslaved African Americans and what their roles were in connection with our farmhouse. In his will, Colonel William Morgan mentioned the first names of the slaves he owned. Some of them might have gone to his son George and eventually to his widow, Drusilla. John Sigler, the farm's tenant manager from 1818 until the year before the Civil War, did not own slaves. We saw an ad in Chapter 5 to sell one of Walter Selby's unnamed slaves. A few letters among the JFH Papers mention slaves, some even in affectionate tones. We also have an 1867 photograph of Mami Sally in Figure 5.9, manifestly a former Selby or Hamtramck family slave. Besides the material on slavery at the farmhouse in Chapter 8, I think this is all we may ever learn about our principal characters' slaves—unless a dedicated researcher takes an interest in delving deeply into deed, census, and tax records.

If living descendants of the Morgan and Selby families come forward who have stories, personal papers, and other documents, we might get a better understanding of the log farmhouse and its earliest years. Descendants of the Morgan family whom I contacted did not have such records or even any knowledge of George Morgan in their ancestry. Local residents surnamed Selby had no connection with Walter Selby's family to their knowledge.

The shortage of information on the people's lives we have looked at here should not be surprising. The hardships of living on the frontier hundreds of years ago could not have allowed much time for reflection or recording daily events much less mundane thoughts and concerns. These people might not have conceived of their lives as particularly interesting or important or thought records of their activities worth saving for people far in the future. They were not living their lives for us to relive them today the way most of us are not documenting our lives to satisfy the curiosity of people several hundred years from now. Nevertheless, I am grateful for what they have left behind. In particular, I appreciate the glimpses into the personal lives of some of our characters that the JFH Papers have afforded.

How many stories could this venerable old home tell us? The history it has seen and withstood is the history of our nation from its creation—built while the land was in principle still under British rule. Several times a day when looking from a window across the gentle hills of the Aspen Pool farm at the changeless vista of the Blue Ridge Mountains, I think how little the view must have changed since George Morgan looked out on it in the 1780's. In a certain way, this connects us across the centuries. What was his life in this house like and the lives of the occupants who followed? Until we can learn more about them, we can only wonder and dream about those families and their long-ago lives.

It is my sincere hope that future owners of the George Morgan House will honor its history and preserve its integrity. I will be grateful if this project has a material impact on realizing this hope. I envision an unwritten pact between generations of owners reaching all the way back to 1780 and continuing far into the distant future to hold this house together and pass on its legacy. We strive to be good stewards of this special place, which fortune has entrusted to us, and consider it a privilege to live in it for a brief period in its long history. With every passing year, preserving homes like ours becomes more critical to our nation as so much of the historical built environment succumbs to the ravages of nature, time, neglect, and ill-considered development.

It is time now to put back to their rest the characters we have met here, briefly revived, and possibly disturbed. I feel I have come to know them personally and will miss their silent company. They have added a rich dimension to this narrative.

Here we will end our story and leave it to future owners, researchers, or students to extend or correct it, or use it as a model to follow related interests. There is no limit to what history has yet to reveal if we only search for it. Professor Richard N. Frye put it well when he wrote:

> [I]t is . . . exhilarating to know that the past, like the natural sciences now and in the future, has no frontiers.[307]

Long may the George Morgan House stand and give future generations shelter and inspiration for centuries to come!

---

307 Frye, Richard N., *The Heritage of Persia*, The New American Library, 1963, 22.

APPENDIX A 18TH- AND 19TH-CENTURY SELBY DEED EXTRACTS[308]

1. **1797–1798 – from Shepherd to Selby** *(assumed to be Abraham Shepherd to Walter B. Selby)*

    *   Deed Book 14, Page 306, Berkeley County.
    *   *This deed was for a lease, but since this deed book is lost—believed burned or stolen during the Civil War—the date, parcel, and amount of rent are unknown. Only the deed book index survived. Since Thomas Shepherd died in 1776, the Shepherd of this deed was one of his descendants, possibly Abraham. Because of the Shepherd name, the lease was probably for a lot or house in Shepherdstown, which could have been the location of the Selby residence or the Selby dry goods store. Walter Selby had run his business since at least 1795, substantiated by the book of his accounts held by the Historic Shepherdstown Museum.*

2. **April 28, 1800 – from Rawleigh** *(Colonel William Morgan's son)* **and Lydia** *(Liddy)* **Morgan to Walter B. Selby**

    *   Deed Book 16, Pages 267–268, Berkeley County.
    *   Consideration of £691 4s.
    *   This parcel contained 85 acres "and all houses, buildings, orchards, ways, waters, water courses, profits, commodities, hereditaments, and appurtenances" belonging to it, and was bounded in part by Abraham, George, and Zachariah (Zacheus) Morgan's lands, among others.
    *   *The words in quotations are common boilerplate language in deeds of this era and do not mean that the land had any or all the characteristics named. This deed could point to the original owner of the log farmhouse, as the three named abutters were all sons of Colonel William Morgan from whose 1788 will each received the 200 acres on which they then lived. At least one of these 200-acre tracts could have included our log farmhouse. The farmhouse stands on the elder Morgan's 1756 land grant of 300 acres, which he*

---

augmented by adding several other sizable land grants in the same area. Any part of his three sons' 200-acre inherited tracts could have been part of any one or more of Colonel Morgan's land grants. Therefore, we cannot make a direct connection by way of this deed between the log farmhouse and the inherited farms of these sons of Colonel Morgan. This purchase was Walter B. Selby's first in a series of acquisitions from the descendants of Colonel William Morgan, which he eventually amassed to form a sizable tract a mile or two southeast of Shepherdstown.

- *This tract was part of a 569 ¾-acre remainder tract devised in Colonel William Morgan's will and sold by executor Abraham Morgan to Rawleigh Morgan on the exact same date of this deed.*

- *Knowing the names of the owners of adjoining Morgan-owned lands mentioned in this deed, I was able to position this 85-acre parcel on a current map by using web-based software.*

3. **December 22, 1802 – from Rawleigh** *(Colonel William Morgan's son)* **and Lydia** *(Liddy)* **Morgan to Walter B. Selby**

   - Deed Book 2, Pages 8–9, Jefferson County.
   - Consideration of $200.
   - This parcel included 5.5 acres and adjoined other lands of Walter B. Selby.
   - This deed was also for part of a larger tract Abraham Morgan conveyed to Rawleigh Morgan on April 28, 1800.
   - *The larger tract must have been the 569 ¾-acre tract referred to in the April 28, 1800 deed (No. 2).*
   - *There is no clue in the deed whether this parcel could have encompassed the log farmhouse. I confirmed that it did not when I plotted it on a current map.*

4. **August 31, 1804 – from Christopher and Mary Orendorf to Walter B. Selby**

   - Deed Book 2, Pages 329–333, Jefferson County.
   - Consideration—the highest bid of $901.
   - This deed is for part of Lot No. 34 in Shepherdstown on the north side of East German Street—the deed gives boundary lengths and

names of abutting owners and streets.

- Abraham Shepherd had a mill on Lot No. 35 to the west of Lot. No. 34. The present-day Town Run still flows through Lot No. 35. Abraham Shepherd kept an easement on Lot No. 34 to allow clearing out the tailrace of his mill.

- The deed mentions two alleys—Clinton's Alley running behind Lot No. 34 from Princess Street and Entler's Alley running along the side lot line from German Street. This deed included a small piece of ground within the intersection of these two alleys for Walter Selby's free ingress and regress from Lot. No. 34 and for the use of the citizens of the town.

- *The deed mentions no existing structures on the lot—although one source notes that Walter Selby might have rented the store he bought in 1804, presumably through this deed. Initially, I thought the store was in the stone house that was formerly the Henry Cookus home, the fourth building to the west of Princess Street.[309] Now I believe that it was on the site of the Selby-Lambright-Reinhart Building to the west of the stone house.[310] Both these buildings stood on Lot No. 34. The fire of 1912 destroyed at least the third and fourth buildings west of Princess Street.*

- *Walter Selby had been leasing property in Shepherdstown as proven by Deed No. 1 noted above. It is possible that the property conveyed by this deed could have been the same one leased under Deed No. 1. If the stone house on Lot No. 34 was the Cookus home, Henry Cookus could have sold it to Abraham Shepherd before renting it to Walter Selby and later selling it to the Orendorfs. But this is unlikely because I believe Selby's building was not of stone but of brick as I told in Chapter 5.*

5. March 21, 1809 – from John Stip Jr. and Eve Stip to Walter B. Selby

- Deed Book 5, Pages 224–227, Jefferson County.
- Consideration of $2,878.
- This parcel contained 101 acres, 1 rood, and 13 poles, and was part of a larger tract conveyed to John Stip Jr. by Benjamin, Sarah,

---

309 "The Shepherdstown of Philip Adam Entler," *Spirit of Jefferson Farmer's Advocate*, October 9, 1986, 10.

310 Price, 69.

and Margaret Halsey on October 27, 1791. It was bounded by tracts owned by Linnean Turner, John Stip, Anthony Turner, George Powell, and Benjamin Foreman.

- *I could not plot this parcel on a current map.*

6. September 20, 1810 – from Rawleigh and Elizabeth Morgan to Walter B. Selby

- Deed Book 6, Pages 168–170, Jefferson County.
- Consideration of $(amount left blank).
- This parcel held half of Lot No. 27 and one-third of Lot No. 26 in Shepherdstown. The deed gives no acreage, only lengths of the lot boundaries. This parcel was the same one conveyed to Rawleigh Morgan by Cornelius and Hanna Wynkoop on February 27, 1800.
- *These are the lots where the historic Wynkoop Tavern stands to this day on the south side of East German Street. This place is where generations of the Selby and Hamtramck families lived.*
- *Rawleigh must have married Elizabeth after his first wife Lydia's death, although I could not verify when Lydia died.*

7. January 14, 1811 – from Peter Hoover to Walter B. Selby

- Deed Book 6, Pages 389–391, Jefferson County.
- Consideration of $326.
- This parcel contained 9 acres, 1 rood, and 10 poles. It was part of a larger tract conveyed to Peter Hoover by Adam and Margaret Keplinger on April 7, 1810. It was bounded by tracts owned by Walter B. Selby, heirs of George Morgan, John Showman, and Peter Hoover.
- *It is possible to plot this parcel on a current map, although I did not. It did not include our log farmhouse, as is clear from Deed No. 8.*
- *This parcel was one that Walter B. Selby was assembling to form a large farm of adjoining tracts southeast of Shepherdstown.*
- *Interestingly, Peter Hoover signed this deed in old-style German cursive script.*

8. **October 25, 1811 – from Rawleigh Morgan Jr.** *(George Morgan's son)* **to Walter B. Selby**

- Deed Book 7, Page 164, Jefferson County.
- Consideration of $2,333.33.
- This deed was for an undivided one-third part of a parcel consisting of 200 acres near Shepherdstown adjoining lands of Walter B. Selby, John Showman, Daniel Staley, the heirs of Zacheus Morgan, and others. This land was the same 200 acres with improvements devised to George Morgan, deceased, by his father, Colonel William Morgan, by his will dated September 9, 1788.
- *George Morgan was the father of Rawleigh Morgan Jr. I do not understand why Rawleigh Morgan Jr. was a "Jr.," if he was George Morgan's son. However, Rawleigh Jr. did have an uncle named Rawleigh, one of Colonel Morgan's sons. I believe Rawleigh Morgan Jr. is the same person some sources refer to as Raleigh Morgan. One or the other name is probably misspelled in the records.*
- *Two other children of George Morgan sold the remaining two-thirds interest in this tract to Walter Selby by way of Deeds No. 14 and No. 15.*
- *This deed refers to the 200 acres and improvements Colonel William Morgan passed on to his son George and "upon which he now lives," as written in the father's will. Therefore, there must have been a house on this 200-acre parcel as early as or more likely earlier than 1788. The deed also implies that George Morgan's son, Rawleigh Jr., received this parcel from his father's estate. Nevertheless, I found no recorded will, appraisal, settlement of an estate, or deed of George Morgan's conveying this parcel to Rawleigh Morgan Jr. either in Berkeley or in Jefferson Counties after his death in 1796.*
- *The deed gives no metes and bounds. It only refers to Colonel Morgan's will for a more particular description of the tract. But Colonel Morgan's will only mentions one adjoining owner, Abraham Morgan, and it gives no metes and bounds. These terms make it impossible without more information to plot this parcel and to try to position it on a present-day map to confirm that the log farmhouse lies within it. I found no other deeds or legal documents that give a*

more detailed description of George Morgan's land.

- Conveniently, I was able to plot the 569 ¾-acre remainder tract from Colonel William Morgan's will mentioned in Deed No. 2 using free online software entitled Plat Plotter 1.42.5.[311] I have not extracted the deed for the remainder tract, dated April 28, 1800, as Walter Selby was not a party to it. It is in Berkeley County Deed Book 16, Page 335, and bears the same date as Deed No. 2.

- Colonel William Morgan's surviving executor, Abraham Morgan, sold the 569 ¾-acre remainder tract from his father's estate twelve years after his death when its lease was out and divided the proceeds among Colonel Morgan's children. Abraham sold the tract to the highest bidder—his brother, Rawleigh.

- The April 28, 1800 deed to the 569 ¾-acre remainder tract is critically important to working out the boundaries of George Morgan's tract because it mentions his heirs as the adjoining landowners along several of its borders. It also used a beginning point in Bullskin Road, now the Shepherdstown Pike, which I was able to pinpoint on a modern map. Some of its boundaries also run along other ancient roads, which still exist.

- At first, I could not get a plot of the remainder tract to make physical sense. Its beginning and ending points were thousands of feet apart, and certain boundaries seemed to be at odd angles or in unlikely locations. When Rawleigh Morgan began selling off pieces of this tract over the next few years, the maps I plotted from deeds associated with those sales did not line up with a plot of the parent 569 ¾-acre tract I had laid out. After studying my plots of these tracts and comparing them with the 1852 S. Howell Brown map, a modern-day property tax map, and satellite maps on Google Earth, I saw some exciting possibilities. When I switched the direction of one of the parent tract's metes from "east" to "west" without changing the degrees of the angle, one of its boundaries matched up perfectly with one of the daughter tract's boundaries. Another of the parent tract's boundaries looked like it closely matched the angle and length of one of the other daughter tracts' boundaries, but it was over 3,000 feet too far to the east. I realized that the transcriber of the parent April

---

311 Rushton, Jason, "Plat Plotter 1.42.5." Retrieved from http://platplotter.appspot .com/

28, 1800 deed had left out an entire boundary. Once I made these two corrections and replotted the 569 ¾-acre tract, it fell into correct alignment with the daughter tracts.

- *As soon as I had this large tract in place on the map, I could infer the boundaries of George Morgan's tract with near complete certainty. The southern and eastern boundaries of George Morgan's tract correspond to borders of the 569 ¾-acre tract. The April 28, 1800 deed describes both these two boundaries as being in line with the land of George Morgan's heirs. I assumed the northern and western boundaries of George Morgan's land were present-day Engle Molers Road and Shepherdstown Pike—both are ancient roads—except for a cutout area immediately southeast of their intersection. The cutout area corresponds to the part of the Springdale Farm property that crosses to the west side of Shepherdstown Pike on the 1852 tax map. This land was owned earlier by Colonel William Morgan, and I reasoned that it had been intact in the early 1800's as it still was in 1852.*

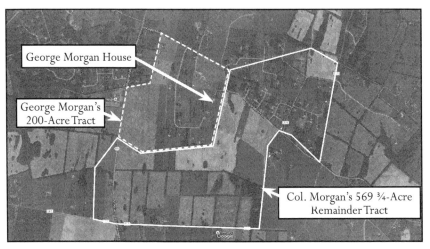

FIGURE A.1 Inferred boundaries (dashed) of George Morgan's 200-acre tract. *Credit: Joseph Goss and Eric D. Goss.*

- *The illustration in Figure A.1 shows the boundaries of the tracts described above. I took scaled measurements from the plot I had made of George Morgan's tract and estimated the area they defined to be roughly 200 acres. The map also shows that our log farmhouse was within George Morgan's land.*

- *It is interesting how many of the lot boundaries of the late 1700's still conform to modern-day roads, property boundaries, and fence lines on satellite maps.*

- *Based on this evidence and other documentation I presented in Chapter 5, I conclude that our log farmhouse was indeed George Morgan's house.*

9. **September 1, 1812 – from John Stip Jr. and Eve Stip to Walter B. Selby**

- Deed Book 7, Pages 321–323, Jefferson County.
- Consideration of $40 per acre *(about $7,250 in total)*.
- This parcel was located about two and a half miles from Shepherdstown, contained 181 acres, 2 roods, and 37 poles, and bordered the properties of James S. Lane, Anthony Turner, and others. It was part of a parcel conveyed to John Stip Jr.'s father by Benjamin, Sarah, and Margaret Halsey on June 17, 1785, and part of another tract conveyed to John Stip Jr.'s father by Williamson, etc., on April 25, 1796.
- *Based on the names of adjoining landowners this parcel abutted other parcels Walter Selby was assembling southeast of Shepherdstown.*

10. **January 8, 1813 – William Morgan Jr.** *(son of Zacheus Morgan, deceased)* **to Walter B. Selby**

- Deed Book 7, Pages 400–402, Jefferson County.
- Consideration of $1,800.
- This parcel contained 50 acres and was part of a larger tract of 200 acres handed down to Zacheus Morgan by his father, Colonel William Morgan, through his 1788 will.
- *The 200-acre tract is where Zacheus lived in 1788, according to his father's will. From Deed No. 8 we learn that Zacheus was already deceased in 1811.*
- This parcel was subject to the dower right of William Morgan Jr.'s widowed mother, Margaret Morgan, for the rest of her life.
- *A dower right is an interest in the real estate of a deceased husband given by law to his widow during her life.*
- *The deed gives no location, boundaries or adjoining owners. However,*

I believe this parcel also abutted the other tracts Walter Selby was assembling southeast of Shepherdstown.

11. May 1, 1813 – John and Catherine Wingard to Walter B. Selby

- Deed Book 8, Pages 104–106, Jefferson County.
- Consideration of $1,100.
- This parcel consisted of part of Lot. No. 35 in Shepherdstown bounded by German Street; Lot No. 34 *(owned by Walter B. Selby)*; a lot where a still stood *(probably the rest of Lot. No. 35)* belonging to Abraham Shepherd; and an 11–foot wide alley to the rear. Abraham and Eleanor Shepherd conveyed this parcel to John and Catherine Wingard on May 24, 1810.
- *This lot abutted Lot No. 34, where Walter Selby had his dry goods business.*

12. February 4, 1814 – from Simon Morgan *(son of Zacheus Morgan, deceased)* to Walter B. Selby

- Deed Book 8, Pages 283–284, Jefferson County.
- Consideration of $1,616.67.
- Simon Morgan was then living in Philadelphia.
- This parcel contained 50 acres and was part of an undivided tract of 200 acres passed on to Zacheus Morgan by his father, Colonel William Morgan, through his 1788 will.
- This parcel was subject to the dower right of Simon Morgan's widowed mother, Margaret Morgan, for the rest of her life.
- *This deed gives no location, boundaries, or adjoining owners. I suspect this parcel was also adjacent to the other tracts Walter Selby was assembling southeast of Shepherdstown.*

13. June 8, 1815 – from Peter Hoover, deceased, to Walter B. Selby

- Deed Book 9, Pages 100–102, Jefferson County.
- Consideration of $70 per acre *($13,903.75 in total)*.
- This parcel contained 198 acres, 2 roods, and 20 poles, about one mile from Shepherdstown, and was created out of two separate

tracts. Adam and Margaret Keplinger conveyed one of these tracts to Peter Hoover on April 7, 1810, about 9 acres of which Walter Selby later purchased from him on January 14, 1811 (Deed No. 7). Abraham and Elizabeth Buckles conveyed the other separate tract to Peter Hoover on April 1, 1811. The parcel of land granted by this deed bordered the road from Charles Town to Barn's Ford on the Potomac River on one side and Walter Selby's line, Adam Link's lines, John Unsold's line, and Showman's line on other boundaries.

- *This parcel was obviously contiguous with the other tracts Walter Selby was assembling southeast of Shepherdstown, authenticated by the adjoining property owners' names, including Walter Selby. Given all the information this deed contains, it would be possible to plot and place this tract on a current map.*

14. September 29, 1815 – from Van Morgan *(George Morgan's son)* to Walter B. Selby

- Deed Book 9, Pages 186–187, Jefferson County.
- Consideration of $5,000.
- The deed identified Van Morgan as a son, heir, and representative of George Morgan.
- It transferred an undivided one-third part of a 200-acre parcel. This land was the same 200 acres devised to George Morgan, deceased, by his father, Colonel William Morgan, through his will of 1788.
- *The description of the parcel conveyed in this deed matches that in the October 25, 1811 deed (No. 8).*

15. April 6, 1817 – from James and Lydia Morgan McCauley to Walter B. Selby *(Lydia was George Morgan's daughter)*

- Deed Book 10, Pages 70–71, Jefferson County.
- Consideration of $5,000.
- This deed is for an undivided one-third part of a 200-acre parcel Lydia Morgan inherited from her father George Morgan who received the same by inheritance from his father, Colonel William Morgan, in 1788 subject to the dower of Drusilla Morgan Thornburg, the remarried widow of George Morgan.

- *The description of the parcel conveyed in this deed matches those in the October 25, 1811, and September 29, 1815 deeds (No. 8 and No. 14), and is thus the last one-third part of George Morgan's 200-acre home place bought by Walter Selby. The entire 200-acre parcel cost Walter Selby a total of $12,333.33 over a five-and-a-half-year period.*

16. April 2, 1818 – from Joel Morgan *(son of Zacheus Morgan, deceased)* to Walter B. Selby

- Deed Book 10, Pages 365–366, Jefferson County.
- Consideration of $3,500.
- This deed was for an undivided ¼ part (50 acres) of a 200-acre parcel inherited by Zacheus Morgan from his father, Colonel William Morgan, through his will of 1788.
- *I suspect this parcel was also adjacent to the other tracts Walter Selby was assembling southeast of Shepherdstown.*

17. May 3, 1819 – from Eleanor Morgan *(daughter of Zacheus Morgan, deceased)* to Walter B. Selby

- Deed Book 11, Page 31, Jefferson County.
- Consideration of $(amount left blank).
- This deed was for an undivided ¼ part (50 acres) of a 200-acre parcel inherited by Zacheus Morgan from his father, Colonel William Morgan, through his will of 1788.
- *Together with Deed Nos. 10, 12, and 16, this deed closes out the sale of Zacheus Morgan's 200-acre tract. His house was somewhere on it. Therefore, Walter Selby bought both George and Zacheus Morgan's dwellings, but I have not figured out where Zacheus's stood or if it still stands.*
- *This Eleanor Morgan is not to be confused with Eleanor Morgan, the daughter of Colonel William Morgan and wife of Walter B. Selby.*
- *I suspect this parcel was also adjacent to the other tracts Walter Selby was assembling southeast of Shepherdstown.*

18. August 19, 1820 – from Drusilla Morgan Thornburg *(widow of George Morgan)* to Walter B. Selby

- Deed Book 11, Pages 260–261, Jefferson County.
- Consideration of $1.
- Drusilla Morgan Thornburg released all her dower right in the one-third part of the undivided 200-acre parcel her son, Van Morgan, transferred to Walter Selby by the September 29, 1815 deed (No. 14).
- *The 1815 deed does not mention any dower right for Drusilla Morgan.*
- *This deed could suggest that Drusilla might have lived in our house after George Morgan's death in 1796 until 1820 even though she had remarried twice during those years. How did this affect Walter Selby's ownership? A dower right usually gave a widow income from the property for the rest of her life. However, if she occupied our property until 1820, her occupancy might have been her dower benefit.*
- *John Sigler was the farmhouse tenant from about 1818 to 1860 as told in Chapter 7. This would conflict with Drusilla staying on at our farmhouse till 1820; however, there could have been another house on the farm, such as the Red Pump farmhouse, which Drusilla could have occupied. I cannot resolve this discrepancy without more information.*
- *I do not know when Drusilla died, but she was living at least until 1824, as confirmed by Deed No. 21.*

19. January 19, 1822 – from Thomas Griggs Jr. to Walter B. Selby and Robert Worthington

- Deed Book 11, Pages 457–458, Jefferson County.
- This deed is a claim for the right to sell to the highest bidder a 120-acre tract of land on the road from Charles Town to Lee Town sold to Samuel and Elizabeth Rupell by deed dated January 31, 1818, upon which the Rupells defaulted.
- *It appears that Selby and Worthington were lenders to the Rupells for this tract. Since this deed does not concern a land purchase by Selby, it does not interest us further. I include it here to present a record of all deeds that name Walter Selby as a grantee and to give a sense of*

the type of financial deals he engaged in besides his own real estate purchases.

20. February 9, 1822 – from Matthew Ranson to Walter B. Selby and Robert Worthington

- Book 11, Pages 456–457, Jefferson County.
- This deed is a trust to secure payment for two separate tracts upon which Samuel and Elizabeth Rupell defaulted. One was a 120-acre tract of land on the road from Charles Town to Lee Town. The other contained 80 acres, 2 roods, and 17 poles and was sold to Rupells by deed dated July 23, 1821.
- *The 120-acre tract was possibly the same tract named in Deed No. 19.*
- *It appears that Selby and Worthington were lenders to the Rupells for these tracts. Since this deed does not concern a land purchase by Selby, it does not interest us further. Nevertheless, I include it here for the same reasons as the previous deed.*

21. April 17, 1824 – from Drusilla Morgan Thornburg to Walter B. Selby

- Deed Book 14, Pages 9–10, Jefferson County.
- Consideration of $1.
- Drusilla Morgan Thornburg released all her dower right in the one-third part of the undivided 200-acre parcel James and Lydia Morgan McCauley deeded to Walter Selby in 1817 (Deed No. 15). Her dower right appears in the 1817 deed.
- *Drusilla Thornburg (mother of Lydia Morgan McCauley and George Morgan's widow) was living in Washington County, Maryland, by the date of this deed. Her second husband, surnamed Thornburg, was deceased by this date and her third husband, Charles Williams, must also have been deceased according to the census of 1820 (see Chapter 8). Why did she give up this dower right or the one in Deed No. 18? She was sixty years old in 1824 and would have still needed dower income for the rest of her life.*

22. **April 24, 1832 – from J. R. Douglass, trustee, to Walter B. Selby and Samuel Deitrick, executor of Adam Myers, deceased**

   - Deed Book 17, Pages 323–324, Jefferson County.
   - Consideration of $1,995.
   - This transfer was for the sale of one Negro man (Harry), one woman (Aley), one boy (Thornton), one woman (Ann), and a variety of household articles.
   - This deed contains the following language, which appears bizarre to us today: "To have and to hold the aforesaid slaves and their increase of the families thereof, and the other movable property above described."
   - *The rest of the deed reads much like any other real estate deed. Although this deed does not include a land purchase by Walter Selby, I include it here because of its chilling historical interest. Together with Walter Selby's census information, the 1815 slave advertisement in Chapter 5, and several letters among the JFH Papers, this deed shows how extensive Walter Selby's involvement was in the business of buying and selling human beings.*

23. **August 6, 1832 – from Thomas G. Harris, Norborne B. Robinson, and Abram Hoffman to Walter B. Selby**

   - Deed Book 18, Pages 14–15, Jefferson County.
   - Consideration of $1.
   - This document is a release of Walter Selby from monies borrowed from and owed to Harris, Robinson, and Hoffman for Selby's purchases of the three one-third parts of the 200-acre tract where George Morgan had lived and which he inherited from his father, Colonel William Morgan.
   - *These three one-third parts of the 200-acre tract are the ones conveyed to Walter Selby in deeds dated October 25, 1811 (No. 8), September 29, 1815 (No. 14), and April 6, 1817 (No. 15) and where our farmhouse stands.*

24. **September 29, 1832 – from Walter B. Selby to George Fulk**

   - Deed Book 18, Pages 87–89, Jefferson County.

- No consideration mentioned.
- This is a complicated instrument concerning unpaid debts related to two deeds dated March 21, 1809 (No. 5) and September 1, 1812 (No. 9). A decree of the Winchester Chancery Court sold part of the two tracts conveyed by these deeds to satisfy part of a debt owed to Jacob Morgan *(George Morgan's cousin)*. The decree states that the rest of the two tracts can either be put up for sale by this agreement, or leased by Selby to Fulk *(possibly a court-appointed trustee)* for one-half of all the wheat, rye, corn, and every other article raised on the land. In the latter case, Selby had to furnish one-half of all the seed grain and planters that Fulk may choose to use on the property to satisfy the rest of the debt.
- *See pp. 104–105 for more discussion about this deed.*

25. April 14, 1834 – from Thomas S. Selby to Walter B. Selby Sr.

- Deed Book 19, Page 303, Jefferson County.
- Consideration of $50.
- This deed was for an undivided one-fifth part of a parcel near Shepherdstown containing 4 acres, adjoining lands of Dr. Henry Boteler and heirs of Saul Bedinger. It is the same land devised to Eleanor Morgan, deceased, mother of Thomas S. Selby, and wife of Walter B. Selby Sr. Colonel William Morgan devised the 4-acre parcel to daughter Eleanor in his 1788 will.

26. April 20, 1836 – from Henry S. Selby to Walter B. Selby Sr.

- Deed Book 21, Pages 197–198, Jefferson County.
- Consideration of $40.
- This deed was for one undivided part of a parcel near Shepherdstown containing 4 acres, adjoining lands of Dr. Henry Boteler and heirs of Saul Bedinger, being the same land devised to Eleanor Morgan, deceased, mother of Henry S. Selby, and wife of Walter B. Selby Sr. Colonel William Morgan devised the 4-acre parcel to daughter Eleanor in his 1788 will.
- *Although it does not specify, this deed might convey another one-fifth part of the four-acre parcel noted in the April 14, 1834 deed (No. 25), since the considerations are similar.*

27. March 19, 1856 – division of the real estate of Walter B. Selby, deceased

- Deed Book 35, Pages 366–367, Jefferson County.

- It is ordered that V. M. Butler, Jacob Line, and Jacob Fulk being first sworn, divide the real estate of Walter B. Selby, deceased, among his heirs and make report thereof according to law.

- Jefferson County to wit: this day personally appeared before the undersigned a justice of the peace for the county previously mentioned V. M. Butler, Jacob Line, and Jacob Fulk who made oath that they would faithfully and to the best of their ability execute this order. Given under my hand this 15th day of March 1856.   J. W. Reynold

- The undersigned as commissioners appointed by the county court of Jefferson have made the following appraisement and division of the real estate of the late Walter B. Selby estate in Shepherdstown. Among the heirs of the estate are Henry Selby, Mrs. (Sally) Hamtramck, Florence and Sarah F. Hamtramck the both commonly called joint heirs of Eliza C. Hamtramck, late wife of John F. Hamtramck and daughter of the late Walter B. Selby.

- The brick storehouse German Street $3,000
  Homestead, Back Lot, and Town Lot   <u>$4,500</u>
  on which there is a dower payable to Mrs. Elizabeth $7,500
  Morgan of $33 $\frac{1}{3}$ per annum during her natural life.

- One third of the above—$2,500 *(to each of the heirs named in the previous paragraph)*

- To Henry Selby $\frac{5}{6}$ of the brick storehouse, warehouse, corn crib & lot $2,500

- Florence & Eliza jointly $\frac{1}{6}$ same $ 500

- Mrs. Hamtramck $\frac{5}{9}$ of the homestead responsible for $\frac{4}{9}$ of Mrs. Morgan's dower interest $\frac{5}{9}$ back lot adjoining and $\frac{5}{9}$ of the pasture lot $2,500

- Florence & Eliza jointly $\frac{4}{9}$ of the homestead responsible for $\frac{4}{9}$ of Mrs. Morgan's dower interest $\frac{4}{9}$ of back lot adjoining homestead $\frac{4}{9}$ pasture lot $2,000
  $\frac{1}{6}$ of storehouse   <u>$ 500</u>
                                                                      $2,500

V. M. Butler
Jacob Line
Jacob Fulk

- In the county court Jefferson County, Virginia. At a court continued and held for said court on the 19th day of March 1856 the preceding division was returned and confirmed by the court and ordered to be recorded.

- *Deed No. 28 explains that Sarah F. Hamtramck is the same person known as Eliza Hamtramck. The 1850 U.S. Census lists parents John F. and Sarah E. Hamtramck living with their children Florence, age thirteen, Eliza, age eleven, and Sallie, age seven. Little Sallie was Colonel Hamtramck's daughter with his third wife, Sarah E. (Sally) Hamtramck. The 1850 census records Sarah F. under her common name of Eliza cited in Deed No. 28. Since Sallie lived until 1862, it is not clear why she was not named an heir in this division of property. Deed No. 29, dated April 1, 1874, uses Florence and Eliza's married names of Florence Shepherd and Sarah (Eliza) Frances Williamson. Thus, we have further confirmation that Florence Shepherd and Eliza Williamson who became co-owners of our farmhouse were daughters of Eliza Claggett Selby Hamtramck and John F. Hamtramck.*

- *This division of property does not mention the George Morgan House and farm; however, they do appear in Deed No. 28.*

28. August 10, 1856 – division of Walter B. Selby's land

- Deed Book 36, Pages 111–113, Jefferson County.

- Division of Walter Selby's real estate as follows:

- In pursuance of an order of the county court of Jefferson County to us directed, we have gone upon the lands of which Walter B. Selby died seized and after a careful examination of the same as to quality, improvements, advantages, and disadvantages attending the same, and with assistance of John P. Rearfott Surveyors, laid off the same as hereinafter specified.

- First—To Henry Selby, we have assigned Lot No. 1 having 184 acres and 31 poles.

- *This is the lot where our log farmhouse stands, as the plan accompanying the deed shows.*

- Second—To Florence and Sarah F. Hamtramck (the latter

commonly called Eliza) we have assigned Lot No. 2 containing 47 acres. We have also assigned to same Lot No. 4, known as the Scrabble Farm having 166 acres, 1 rood, and 32 poles.

- *According to the plan accompanying this division of land, Lot No. 2 adjoins Lot No. 1 and is on the east side of Shepherdstown Pike. The Scrabble Farm is a separate tract to the northwest of Shepherdstown in the Scrabble settlement area. Florence and Sarah F. Hamtramck were daughters of Eliza Claggett Selby Hamtramck and John F. Hamtramck as made clear in Deed No. 27. Eighteen years later in 1874, they appear in Deed No. 29 with their married names of Florence Shepherd and Sarah Frances Williamson as co-owners with Henry Selby of Walter Selby's old brick storehouse and even later in a 1914 deed (No. 31), sixteen years after Henry's death, as co-owners of property that included our log farmhouse. This is solid evidence that these two women inherited the farmhouse and its land from Henry Selby, although I found no documentation of this inheritance.*

- Third – To J. F. Hamtramck and Sarah E., his wife we have assigned Lot No. 3 having 186 acres, 3 roods, and 9 poles. The timber on Lot No. 2 and the timber on Lot No. 3 are hereby reserved in the assignment of those two lots and assigned to Henry Selby, he to have twelve months to cut and remove the same. We have also directed that the fences running parallel or nearly so with the following lines . . . shall be removed thence from; each of the interested to help in removing said fences and when so removed to be equally divided.

- *This division consists of a total of 584 acres of land of which 418 acres relates to the log farmhouse property. The separate so-called Scrabble Farm northwest of Shepherdstown made up the remaining 166 acres. No other children of Walter Selby receive any land in either this division of property or the division of real estate under Deed No. 27. From other sources, we know the years of the deaths of Henry, Eliza, Sarah, William, and Walter Selby Jr. Henry and Sarah were the only ones of these five who outlived their father. We do not know the dates of death of Walter Selby's sons Thomas S., John C., or James M. Selby; however, they also probably predeceased their father having received no inheritance under this division of land or Deed No. 27.*

29. April 1, 1874 – from Henry S. Selby (of Shepherdstown), James and Florence Shepherd (of Shepherdstown), and Luke T. and Sarah Frances Williamson (of Baltimore) to James W. Greenwood

- Deed Book B, Page 17, Jefferson County.
- Consideration of $3,000.
- This deed was for a house and lot on German Street in Shepherdstown bounded by heirs of Robert G. Harper, being the same property assigned to the three grantor parties by the court in dividing the real estate of Walter B. Selby, deceased, on March 19, 1856 *(Deed No. 27)*.
- *This building must be the brick storehouse on German Street mentioned in Deed No. 27, which served as Walter B. Selby's dry goods store on Lots No. 34 and No. 35.*
- *See pp. 69 and 74–75 for further discussion about this deed.*

APPENDIX B 20TH- AND 21ST-CENTURY DEED AND WILL EXTRACTS[312]

30. January 8, 1914 – from Florence Shepherd to Eliza Williamson

- Deed Book 110, Pages 316–317, Jefferson County.

- Consideration of $1.

- Both parties owned equal shares of three parcels known as the Cherry Hill, Red Pump, and Wheatland farms about 2 miles south of Shepherdstown containing a total of 596 acres, 3 roods, and 11 poles. This deed partitions the real estate between the two parties wherein Shepherd grants her full title and interest to Williamson in the part of the land designated as Tract No.1 containing 275 acres, and 25 poles.

- *A plat of Tract No. 1 annexed to the deed shows that it includes our farm, Wheatland, and its farmhouse as does the 1928 Shaw and Whitmer map.*

- *The deed gives no information about how these two women received this real estate, although it had passed to Walter B. Selby's son, Henry S. Selby, in the 1856 division of the father's land found in Deed No. 28. It must have come down to them as an inheritance from Henry S. Selby since they were his nieces and the daughters of Eliza Claggett Selby Hamtramck and John F. Hamtramck. Henry died intestate in 1898 and, as far as I know, owned the farmhouse until his death.*

- *Of the 584 acres listed in the 1856 division of Walter B. Selby's lands (Deed No. 28) 418 contiguous acres lay south of Engle Molers Road on both sides of Shepherdstown Pike and contained the Wheatland, Red Pump, and Cherry Hill farms, although only the Wheatland farmhouse appears on the plat of Tract No. 1. The separate Scrabble Farm property northwest of Shepherdstown having 166 acres made up the rest of the 584 acres. The 418 contiguous acres formed the core of the approximately 596-acre parcel referred to in this deed. Henry S. Selby must have acquired an additional 178 acres adjacent to the 418 acres needed to complete the 596-acre tract*

---

312 Regular font denotes extracted original deed content. Italic font denotes author's comments on the deeds.

sometime after 1856, although I found no deeds to prove this or to show where the 178-acre tract's boundaries ran.

- Deed Book 110, Pages 319–321, also dated January 8, 1914, grants Tract No. 2 to Florence Shepherd. A plat of the 321-acre Tract No. 2 is annexed to the deed.

- *The plat shows the Red Pump and Cherry Hill farmhouses included within it. These two houses also appear on the 1928 Shaw and Whitmer map confirming that they were still standing at least up to that time. Neither one survives today.*

31. April 5, 1921 – From Eliza Williamson to her daughters Florence Williamson Sampson and Gay Selby Williamson

- Deed Book 120, Pages 242–243, Jefferson County.
- Consideration of $10.
- This deed was for a particular parcel of real estate about two miles south of Shepherdstown known as Wheatland farm comprised of about 275 acres. Eliza Williamson and her sister Florence Shepherd had inherited a larger parcel that included this tract from Henry S. Selby. Deed No. 30 divided the larger parcel between Eliza and Florence.

32. August 25, 1930 – Gay Selby Williamson of Baltimore

- Will Book G, Page 430, Jefferson County.
- The deceased leaves the Hamtramck silver and three military commissions of her great-grandfather John Francis Hamtramck to her sister Florence W. Sampson, as well as all the rest and residue of her estate.
- *Although John Francis Hamtramck was Gay Williamson's grandfather, the John Francis Hamtramck named in this will actually refers to his father, Jean-François Hamtramck—sometimes called John Francis Hamtramck (1756–1803)—who also had a military career.*
- She also leaves $1,000 to the Woman's Library of Shepherdstown and $1,000 to the Catholic Church of Shepherdstown.
- *This will transferred Gay Selby Williamson's interest in the Wheatland farm to her sister Florence Williamson Sampson who later*

became Florence W. Clarke. This assumes the farm was part of the residue of Gay's estate, which she received from her mother through Deed No. 31.

- *According to Deed No. 29, Gay Selby Williamson's mother, Eliza Williamson, already lived in Baltimore in 1874, where Gay would have grown up and where we know she died.*

33. June 18, 1946 – From Florence W. Clarke to Howard T. and Mary L. Skinner

- Deed Book 165, Page 284, Jefferson County.
- Consideration of $10.
- This deed was for a tract two miles south of Shepherdstown known as Wheatland farm having 275 acres and 25 perches.
- *This tract was the same land that Eliza Williamson conveyed to her daughters—Florence Williamson Sampson and Gay Selby Williamson—by Deed No. 31. Florence Williamson Sampson later became Florence W. Clarke, the grantor of this deed.*
- Florence W. Clarke inherited this tract from her sister, Gay Selby Williamson *(Deed No. 32).*
- *This deed confirms that our log farmhouse was in the Selby and Hamtramck families continuously from 1811 to 1946—a total of 135 years.*
- *This does not appear to be an arms-length transaction, because of the nominal consideration. As I explained in Chapter 7, the Skinners had been renting the property since 1920, which might have had a bearing on the nominal consideration.*

34. March 12, 1969 – From Mary L. Skinner, widow, Edna S. and Hans Reinheimer, William M. and Winifred Skinner, Imogene S. and John C. Pound, Ada S. and Clarence R. Mills, Howard T. Skinner Jr. and Rebecca Skinner, and John T. Skinner, divorced, to Gilbert P. Wright Jr.

- Deed Book 303, Page 499, Jefferson County.
- Consideration of $73,500.
- This deed was for a significant part of the tract of land about two miles south of Shepherdstown known as Wheatland farm

comprised of 275 acres and 25 perches. The whole tract was the same as once owned by Eliza Williamson (Deed No. 30).

- *A notable error in this deed is the inclusion of the name Eliza Whittington as having received this property on January 8, 1914, via Deed No. 30. It took hours for me to figure out that this was not an additional party to Deed No. 30, but merely a near-total misspelling of one occurrence of Eliza Williamson's name in that deed. There is no Eliza Whittington party to any Jefferson County deeds.*

- *The land this deed transferred excluded certain tracts amounting to about 29 ¼ acres of the original approximately 275-acre farm, but it still included our log farmhouse.*

- *I do not know how the grantors besides Mary Skinner came to their ownership of the property. Some of them are Skinner family members who might have inherited their interests in it from Howard T. Skinner, deceased.*

35. March 13, 2001 – From Gilbert P. and Stacy Wright to Mark Mulligan and David R. Haarberg

- Deed Book 947, Page 169, Jefferson County.
- Consideration of $170,000.
- This deed was for a parcel described as Lot No. 1, Gilbert and Stacy Wright Minor Subdivision, of 10.1999 acres as illustrated by a plat in Jefferson County Plat Book 18, at Page 48.
- *This parcel includes our log farmhouse.*

36. June 3, 2011 – From Mark Mulligan and David R. Haarberg to Joseph and Lynne F. Goss

- Deed Book 1094, Page 661, Jefferson County.
- Consideration of $370,000.
- *This deed was for the same 10.1999-acre parcel conveyed to Mulligan and Haarberg by Gilbert and Stacy Wright via Deed No. 35.*

APPENDIX C MORGAN AND SELBY–HAMTRAMCK FAMILY TREES

FIGURES C.1 AND C.2 represent in part the Morgan and Selby–Hamtramck family trees. Their purpose is to clarify the relationships of the various family members to each other, clear up confusion between people with duplicate names, and show ownership of the farmhouse. They end with the generations that sold the farmhouse out of these families. Some of the Hamtramck family particulars, which I have not found published anywhere else, come from the Hamtramck family tree owned by the Historic Shepherdstown Museum.

Where I show married couples owning the farmhouse, I have included the wives as de facto owners, even though there were no recorded deeds to memorialize the wives' ownership. I have used the proper form of people's names and also included informal and married names where they are appropriate. I have added specific birth and death years if they appear in at least one source.

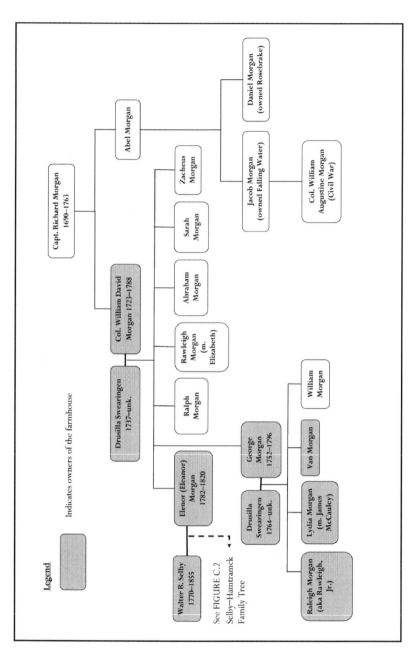

FIGURE C.1 Morgan family tree
Credit: Joseph Goss.

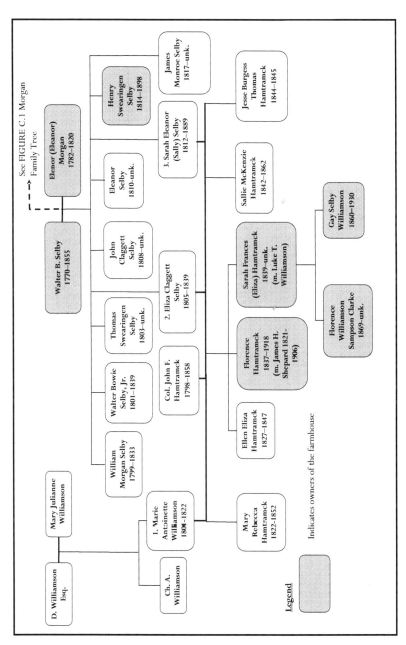

FIGURE C.2 Selby–Hamtramck family tree.
Credit: Joseph Goss.

ABOUT THE AUTHOR

J OE GOSS EARNED a B.S. in mechanical engineering in 1967 from the University of California, Berkeley. He joined the Peace Corps the same year and worked at the Ministry of Agriculture in Kabul, Afghanistan. After Peace Corps, he worked for the U.S. Agency for International Development designing and installing a network of flow gauging stations on the irrigation canals of Helmand and Kandahar Provinces. Returning to California in 1970, Joe met his future wife, Lynne Fleming, of New York. He worked for the U.S. Geological Survey in Eureka and Menlo Park, California, for the next two years.

Author and family—Kim, Lynne, Joe, Eric, Margaux, Heather, Luka, and Angela. *Credit: Joseph Goss.*

Joe earned an M.S. in environmental engineering from Stanford University in 1973. After Stanford, he and Lynne moved to the Boston area where they raised their two children. Joe worked for several New England engineering firms for over two decades, then moved to the Washington, D.C., region. There he worked to rehabilitate the region's aging water and sewer infrastructure for twenty more years, which he continues on a part-time basis. Joe and Lynne divide their time between Shepherdstown, West Virginia, and Gaithersburg, Maryland. They treasure time with their children, their spouses, and grandchildren at the old farmhouse. They also love returning to New England, where they have many dear friends, and traveling to France, to renew bonds with Lynne's family.

INDEX

Made in the USA
Middletown, DE
22 February 2019